Credit Secrets

Book

+ 11 Word Phrase

(2025 Edition)

Financial Mastery Institute

Credit Secrets Bible:

Leverage New, Powerful Insider Tactics, Proven 609 Letter Templates to Master an 800+ FICO Score. Your Path to Boundless Financial Freedom & Unmatched Security.

Financial Mastery Institute

Exclusive Bonuses:
A Surprise Just For You!

We designed this book to be an all-inclusive mentor on your credit improvement journey. But we didn't stop there. To keep you inspired, rewarded and motivated, we've whipped up some exclusively valuable bonuses, crafted just for you!

Navigating along with your credit improvement mission, we understand you need more than just mere information - tools that give you tactical control, and resources that equip you for action.

For this, we provide the perfect accompaniments to your newfound knowledge – a handy **"Credit Score Improvement Checklist"** and six powerful **"609 Letter Templates"**.

To gain immediate access, simply scan the QR code
It's that easy!

Table of Contents

Introduction

Welcome to *Credit Secrets: 2024 Edition - Leverage New, Powerful Insider Tactics & Proven 609 Letter Templates to Master an 800+ FICO Score.* Your Path to Boundless Financial Freedom & Unmatched Security. This guide is your definitive roadmap to navigating the complex terrain of credit scores, lending practices, and financial responsibility. The revelation of credit management techniques found within these pages might just be the key that unlocks your journey to unparalleled financial independence.

Do you feel the shackles of a low FICO score binding your dreams? Maybe, the specter of loan disapproval is casting a dark shadow over your hopes of owning a cozy house or a shiny new car? Or is the strain of high-interest rates and elusive credit opportunities keeping you awake at night? Or perhaps, you're a young adult who is just starting out, teetering on the cusp of the credit universe, embarking upon the quest for financial stability.

If you nodded affirmatively to any of the above, take heart—you are holding the answer to your questions, worries, and anxieties right in your hands.

This book is your trusted, indispensable guide—whether you're a hardworking parent yearning for financial steadiness, a hopeful homeowner grappling with mortgage intricacies, or a motivated young adult ready to build a solid credit foundation. Authored by seasoned professionals, who have walked in your shoes and mastered the labyrinth of credit, lending, and fiscal management, this book is a trove of actionable strategies, powerful secrets, and methodical tactics that span everything there is to master credit and its universe.

Within these pages, you'll uncover empowering insights into FICO scoring algorithms, the muscle memory needed to build a resilient credit foundation, expert ways to dispute inaccuracies and win, rarely-shared loopholes that give you a credit edge, knockout negotiation strategies to conquer debt, and pioneering protection tactics to guard your score from theft, among many others. It's like having your personal credit consultant, available 24/7 at your beck and call.

But this book is more than just a guide - it's an awakening. Once you've seen what's possible, once you've tasted the liberty that comes with a powerful FICO score and secure financial health, there's no turning back. You will be equipped with the knowledge, tools, and understanding that only a fraction of people have – an insider's view into the machinations of credit and financial freedom.

Empowerment, assurance, control over your financial destiny— that's what you seek, and that's precisely what "Credit Secrets" promises. Spanning a vast array of topics, from the very basics of credit scores to advanced strategies deployed by credit veterans, this book is a one-stop-shop for your credit mastery.

We invite you to not just read this book, but to immerse yourself in it. To challenge yourself by applying these tactics, to celebrate each win, and to learn from every stumble. You're not just turning a page here; you are turning a new leaf towards a future unburdened by credit constraints and blooming with financial prosperity.

If you ever dreamed of an 800+ FICO score, a life devoid of high-interest rate nightmares, a future where loans are not roadblocks but stepping stones to progress, then this book is your first step towards making those dreams a reality. Grab this chance, step onto the ladder of financial security, and experience the unmatched tranquility that only comes with a sense of control over your destiny.

Your journey towards financial freedom and unmatched security starts now...

Chapter 1:

Decoding the Mysteries: Demystifying Credit Scores & FICO

1.1 The Genesis of Credit Scores

In the sweeping story of credit history, no chapter is arguably more momentous than the birth of the credit score. This humble three-digit number represents more than a mere summation of data - it encapsulates the financial life story of each hard-working parent seeking stability, each young adult looking to stand on their own financial feet, and the myriad of aspiring homeowners dreaming of their perfect house. Knowing that this small numerical representation holds sway over their ability to secure loans or take advantage of quality credit, it's therefore crucial for us to delve into the genesis of credit scores.

The dawn of credit assessment began earlier than you might think. In the 1800s, merchants often extended credit to customers based on personal knowledge. But as towns grew into bustling cities and personal relationships faded, the need for a systematic credit evaluation method became apparent. The concept of credit reporting emerged, with companies collecting financial information to assess a person's creditworthiness. However, this system was far from perfect. The lack of standardization meant that different creditors could have vastly divergent opinions on a person's creditworthiness.

Then, along came two businessmen named Bill Fair and Earl Isaac. In the 1950s, they dared to beg the question- what if a consistent, impartial mathematical model could predict an individual's creditworthiness? They postulated that a score derived from various significant variables like an individual's payment history, amounts owed, and length of credit history, could accurately depict one's credit risk.

Fair and Isaac initiated a revolution grounded in this idea, one that would change the landscape of credit and finance forever. They formed Fair, Isaac, and Company, which is now internationally recognized as FICO. Their goal was ambitious, democratizing access to credit by using a numerical score based on data-driven creditworthiness. This score became the heart of their predictive analytics software sold to lenders.

The introduction of such a system streamlined the credit evaluation process, providing a measurable, unbiased assessment of any individual's credit risk. With each person now represented by a three-digit score, lenders could swiftly and fairly make credit decisions. This transformative approach leveled the playing field, as credit decisions were no longer influenced by personal bias or incomplete data.

Decades later, the FICO Score is a universally recognized measure of creditworthiness in America. Its creation dismantled barriers and unlocked financial possibilities for countless people. Coming to understand your credit score isn't merely about absorbing data and mathematical models; it's about honoring a movement that revolutionized the world of finance and made it accessible to regular folks seeking financial stability.

In this journey towards a better credit score, recognizing the history and purpose of the credit score is paramount. It will serve as your guiding principle to navigate the complex world of credit. Just as the credit score was created with fairness in mind, you are now armed with the knowledge to strive for your deserved financial fairness.

Your credit score is not merely a reflection of numbers and financial behavior; it's an emblem of personal financial growth, resilience, and confidence. And just as Bill Fair and Earl Isaac took this monumental step many years ago, you too are standing on the precipice of your journey to financial empowerment.

Today's credit score underscores the modern financial experience. Gaining a deeper understanding and appreciation of its inception story provides not only historical context but more importantly, motivation. Grasping the origins of credit scoring provides a profound reflection on the transformative power this score has on everyday lives. It lays the groundwork for the chapters to come as you journey to step out of the shadows of financial insecurity and step into the light of financial stability. A simple score it may seem, but understanding its genesis unveils its significant influence on modern-day finance and a person's journey towards financial freedom.

1.2 How FICO Scores Work: An Overview

At first glance, the intricacies involved in calculating a three-digit credit score might seem like dispatches from an arcane world. However, behind those numbers, lies an intelligible logic backed with comprehensible science. To better understand how FICO Scores work, it is essential to take a peek behind the curtain and decode the mysteries of credit scoring.

Marvel at the Marvel of Mathematics

Not unlike a grand symphony composed of distinct yet harmonious partitions, the FICO score is an amalgamation of separate credit-related components enlacing together to weave an individual's credit story. Your FICO credit score is a number ranging from 300 to 850 calculated using five key areas: payment history, amounts owed, length of credit history, new credit, and types of credit used. A higher score is an indication of lesser credit risk, potentially opening the doors to loans and credit with more favorable terms.

Abiding by The Rule of Five

Though the algorithm FICO uses to calculate credit scores is kept exceedingly confidential, they provide broad guidance about the five different factors and their relative weightage:

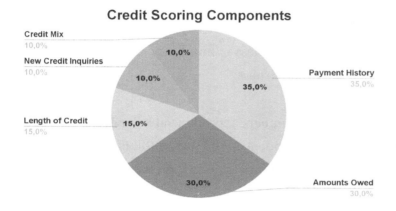

1. Payment History (35%): Emblematic of past reliability, payment history forms the bedrock of your FICO score. Consistently paying bills on time sends a strong signal about your creditworthiness. Late payments, bankruptcy, and other negative elements may hurt your score, reflecting negatively on the element of dependability.

2. Amounts Owed (30%): This factor considers your overall indebtedness, including the number of accounts with outstanding balances and how much of your available credit is in use. Here, high numbers aren't necessarily bad - it hinges on the context. High usage compared to your credit limit can be a red flag, suggesting you're over-reliant on credit.

3. Length of Credit History (15%): A longer credit history with a good track record can enhance your score. It's worth noting that even people with short credit histories can have high scores, provided other factors play out well.

4. Credit Mix (10%): The diversity of your credit portfolio - credit cards, retail accounts, installment loans, mortgage loans - comes into play. A varied mix highlights your ability to manage different types of credit.

5. New Credit (10%): Several recent applications for new credit may signify increased risk, which could negatively impact your score. However, rate shopping for a single loan should not affect the score significantly.

Intricacies Wrapped in the Numbers

The richness of a FICO score can only be appreciated when you begin to explore the minute details within. It reflects not merely the raw figures, such as how many accounts you have or the sum you owe but also intricate dynamics like the proportion of utilized to available credit, or the frequency and recency of missed payments.

For instance, a single missed payment may fade away in the importance over time if it's an isolated case, surrounded by a consistent pattern of timely payments. Similarly, carrying high balances on a few accounts may be less concerning if your overall utilization rate is low. No single factor or incident will define your score, making it a nuanced, dynamic gauge of creditworthiness.

Factoring in the Individuality

An element of subjectivity permeates the FICO scoring system. The impact of each factor depends on the complete credit profile. For instance, a late payment may have a more pronounced effect on someone with a short credit history than on someone with a more established credit history.

By weaving these intricate elements harmoniously, the FICO score produces a credit annotation of significance. Knowing the components and how they interact not only disentangles the enigma of your credit score but also gives you the keys to proactively shape it.

Building the Pillars of Financial Resilience

In understanding the functionalities of a FICO score, you not only unravel its underpinnings but also soak in valuable insights into credit management. Each of the five crucial components links back to a fundamental aspect of sensible financial behavior – from making timely payments to responsibly managing debt. By understanding these factors, you can develop robust strategies that help elevate your credit score over time.

If we consider the metaphor of a building, your FICO score then would be the architect's sketch, with each credit behavior acting as a foundational pillar. Understanding how these pillars foster the structural integrity of the credit score sketch helps you to reconstruct, reinforce, and re-engineer your financial fortress.

Introducing you to the fascinating world of credit scoring and breaking down factors that typically look daunting, we hope to empower you in managing your credit marine. Factors that affect your score are primarily reflections of your financial behavior, and understanding these allows you to devise an effective action plan. With this knowledge in hand, you embark on a journey from financial insecurity, through the labyrinth of FICO scoring, and towards a high credit score and a brighter financial tomorrow.

1.3 The Importance of Credit Scores

In today's world, your credit score is a bit like an ID card you carry through the financial world. It identifies you, reveals key information about your financial health and signals your trustworthiness to a wide range of potential lenders and creditors. To underestimate the significance of this three-digit number would be to diminish one's understanding of financial dynamics. The importance of credit scores goes beyond just loans and credit cards; it travels across aspects that play a crucial role in your financial journey.

What doors does a credit score unlock?

Your credit score doesn't just determine your financial persona; it profoundly influences the scope and quality of financial opportunities available to you. Consider a young couple, the Smiths, who dream of owning a home. When they apply for a mortgage, their credit score becomes the gatekeeper. A high score might unlock the door to their dreams with a low-interest rate mortgage, while a low score could reduce their chances of approval, or burden them with steeper interest rates. In the same vein, a hopeful entrepreneur looking for a business loan to kick start a venture might find their dreams fueled or foiled by their credit score.

The Interest Rate Riddle

In the vast puzzle of financial management, interest rates are a significant component. High-interest rates can make monthly repayments burdensome, slowing down the pace of debt reduction, and accelerating the cycle of accumulating debt. Here is where your credit score steps in as a decisive factor.

Take for instance, our friend, Mr. Johnson, who decides to finance his brand new vehicle with an auto loan. Had his credit score been strong, he might have enjoyed an attractive rate, with smaller monthly repayments translating to less money spent over the loan's tenure. However, with a mediocre credit score, the interest rate on his auto loan is significantly higher, leading to hefty monthly repayments that leave him feeling financially strained every month. This illustration gives us a glimpse into how a robust credit score fast tracks the journey to debt-free living through lower interest costs.

The Insurance Paradox

Interestingly, the ripple effect of your credit score goes beyond the world of loans and borrowings. It extends to the field of insurance premiums. As unusual as it sounds, many insurance companies use credit-based insurance scores to set premiums. Imagine a cautious lady, Mrs. Adams, seeking to insure her family home. The insurer, as part of the decision-making process, takes a look at her insurance score, which in part is influenced by her credit score.

Unfortunately, Mrs. Adams' credit score isn't sparkling, leading to a lower insurance score, which limps towards a higher home insurance premium. This example highlights how your credit score can implicitly impact your monthly expenditures, making a strong score a desirable trait for ways you may not initially realize.

Job Opportunities and Housing Options

Credit scores might also play a subtle role in your hunt for that perfect job or apartment. Employers, especially those in financial sectors, may use a candidate's credit report as part of their background check. A troubled credit history might raise a red flag, potentially costing job opportunities. Likewise, future landlords might take a peek at your credit report before handing over the keys to that perfect rental home you've been eyeing. While these checks typically look at your report and not your score, they hinge on the same financial behaviors embodied by your credit score.

Here, our friend, Ms. Thompson, an aspiring investment banker, may find her credit score impacting her dream job if potential employers perceive poor credit behavior as unprofessional or irresponsible. The dream rental downtown could also slip beyond reach if her prospective landlord views her low credit score as a sign of potential default in the future.

The Invisible Hand that Guides your Financial Future

In essence, your credit score forms the invisible hand shaping your financial outcomes. The examples we explored above reveal that a high credit score isn't just a number; it's a powerful tool that opens doors to better loan options, preferable interest rates, reduced insurance premiums, and even wider job and housing opportunities. Your credit score's influence stretches out to touch almost every aspect of financial life, amplifying its importance and underscoring the crucial need for individuals to nurture it proactively.

1.4 FICO vs VantageScores: The Key Differences

Decoding the realms of credit scores often feels like traversing an ever-changing labyrinth. The plethora of contrasting information, ambiguous interpretations, and technical champions turn the journey into a puzzling challenge. While FICO and VantageScore credit scores are two of the most prominent players in credit score arena, deciphering their differences bears crucial significance for understanding and enhancing credit health.

To FICO or VantageScore: The Tale of Two Models

The evolution of credit scores witnessed the inception of two powerful systems: FICO (Fair Isaac Corporation), the brainchild introduced in 1989, and VantageScore, the model born in 2006 as a collaborative effort among the three major credit bureaus. Fundamentally, although both systems aim at predicting a borrower's credit risk, the disparities in their methodologies and calculation principles can lead to vastly different scores for the same individual.

The Genesis of FICO and VantageScore

The critically acclaimed FICO model, arising from a statistical procedure to assess credit risk, has over the years fortified its cherished position in the lending universe. Fostered by pioneers who were determined to systemize credit reporting, FICO has stood the test of time with its progressive versions and evolving models, currently FICO 8 being most widely used.

VantageScore, a creation tailored by Experian, TransUnion, and Equifax, was launched years later with an aspiration to present a unified, competition-worthy counterpart to the FICO dominion. Its consistency across credit bureaus and a more forgiving nature towards occasional late payments have emerged as selling points that enrich its appeal. The latest version of this model, VantageScore 4.0, has gained momentum for scoring almost 40 million more people than FICO, making inroads into a segment often neglected by the older model.

The Diversity in Score Ranges

Both systems churn out a three-digit number as the final credit score, but their respective score ranges differ, potentially causing confusion during comparison. FICO scores fall within 300 to 850, whereas VantageScore operates on a similar yet distinct scale of 501 to 990. The variance in scale fortifies the argument against comparing apples to oranges, emphasizing the importance of using the correct range and score model for a proper appraisal of credit health.

Secrets Encased in Calculations

The factors employed in calculations by FICO and VantageScore further contribute to their divergences. FICO scores are determined by five key components: payment history, credit utilization, credit age, types of credit, and recent credit inquiries, each assigned a percentage weightage. An excellent FICO score signifies a solid track record of timely payments, prudent utilization of available credit, a well-aged credit profile, a healthy blend of credit types, and minimal recent credit inquiries.

VantageScore, on the other hand, operates on a six-factor model, introducing 'Available Credit' as a separate component, echoing its emphasis on credit utilization. Even the weightage distribution for these factors is shrouded in more ambiguity under VantageScore, contributing to the estimation uncertainty and signaling a more dynamic, behavior-centric model.

Twilight Zoning the Thin Files

Arguably, the most defining edge VantageScore holds against FICO lies in its more inclusive model, offering a scoring solution for thin-file consumers. Thin-file credit users, often young adults or immigrants who lack substantial credit history, find themselves in a disconcerting twilight zone where traditional models like FICO fail to score them. VantageScore, with its ability to score anyone who has reported credit activity within the last two years, presents a ray of hope for these consumers, forging an empowering, inclusive route in credit score landscape.

The Unseen Chasms

While the highlighted points explain the key differences between FICO and VantageScore, the chasms between these models run deeper and off the beaten path. The models' idiosyncrasies concerning medical debts, public records, and collection accounts, to name a few, further delineate their unique personas. Mastery over these traits unlocks a strategic trove of credit score management, empowering individuals to wield their knowledge for better scores.

Deciphering credit scores can feel like navigating a maze, but understanding the distinct personas of FICO and VantageScore can light the way. The contrasts in score ranges, calculation components, inclusivity, and nuanced policies signal that FICO and VantageScore, while similar on surface, exhibit distinctly different characteristics beneath the surface.

Chapter 2:
Introducing the Credit Score Champions: Your Journey Begins Here

2.1 The Hallmarks of a Credit Score Champion

A credit score champion is a person who can navigate the complex labyrinth of credit health and achieve extraordinary success. Not only do they possess an impressive credit score, but their expertise in managing credit has granted them an empowered and financially stable life. With financial freedom at their fingertips, credit score champions enjoy the benefits of an 800+ FICO score, and beyond, that opens doors to opportunities previously shrouded by limited financial prospects. For those in the pursuit of becoming crediting score champions, there are specific hallmarks that define and distinguish them from others.

Keen Understanding of the Credit Landscape

A credit score champion has an in-depth knowledge of how credit scores work, as well as the intricate nuances of FICO and VantageScores. This comprehension empowers credit score champions to understand the methodologies and calculation principles unique to these credit scoring systems. Familiarity with credit history, credit utilization, types of credit, and recent credit inquiries enables them to remain in control of their credit health despite the disparities and complexities presented by different models.

A Solid Foundation

A champion has a clean, strong, and stable foundation in their credit profile. They understand the importance of credit report components and recognize their impact on final scores. A credit score champion's credit report shows a consistent history of timely payments, low credit utilization, diverse forms of credit, and minimal recent inquiries. A concrete foundation indicates reliability and trustworthiness to lenders and serves as an essential building block for a successful credit journey.

Strong Financial Discipline

With a keen awareness of the potential pitfalls in the credit world, champions possess the discipline and diligence to maintain strong financial habits. They regularly monitor their financial activities and credit utilization, efficiently manage existing credit accounts, and prevent excessive debt accumulation. Budgeting, tracking expenses, and employing prudent financial practices form the cornerstone of their credit-based lifestyle, protecting them from the repercussions of poor credit.

Recovery and Adaptability

Mishaps may occur, and even the most accomplished credit score champions face setbacks. However, their ability to rapidly identify and rectify credit issues distinguishes them from the rest. Whether it is through expert negotiation techniques to settle debts, shrewd credit disputes, or other advanced strategies, credit champions turn adversity into opportunity. By employing efficient credit rebuilding processes and learning from past experiences, they continuously refine and optimize their credit management techniques.

Staying Informed and Up-to-Date

In the ever-evolving realm of credit scoring, champions remain vigilant in staying informed about industry developments, policy changes, and technological advancements. Their familiarity with credit scoring models, as well as the legal rights granted to borrowers, enables them to make informed decisions and effectively wield their knowledge in negotiations and disputes. Adapting to the shifting financial landscape, they consult credit monitoring and management tools and services, utilizing user-friendly dashboards to understand their credit standing effortlessly.

Financial Empowerment and Education

Champions are deeply invested in the pursuit of financial literacy. By continually enhancing their knowledge about credit scores, they not only elevate their financial stability but also strive to share their expertise with others in their community. Recognizing the importance of assisting others in their credit journeys, champions often engage in educating people about credit health best practices, inspiring friends and family members to emulate their success in mastering the credit universe.

2.2 Adopting the Champions Attitude

Embracing the credo of a champion requires an understanding that success is an attitude. The journey from financial setbacks to a high credit score isn't exclusively about improving numbers; it's an intricate tapestry of mindset transformation, you will notice, takes precedence. The mindset of a champion is shaped by determination and resilience—qualities perceived as they lean into financial literacy, harness tools, and work towards a future grounded in stability and prosperity.

The Resilient Mindset

When forming a champions attitude, resilience is the linchpin. It's a journey where your resolve will, at times, be tested. Perhaps, you received a decline on an important loan application. Or, an unexpected medical bill pummeled your finances. You might even still be trying to crawl out from a debt pit. A champion understands that such challenges are not the end of the journey; they are stepping stones to ascend towards the zenith of financial freedom. Resilience triggers the ability to bounce back—a comeback using the setbacks as fuel to propel towards the goal.

Deriving Strength from Vulnerabilities

Credit score champions perceive periods of financial vulnerability as stages of growth. Challenges are faced head-on, each experience embraced as an opportunity to learn and grow. Many champions have stories that echo scenarios of financial despair. Today, these past disappointments are narrated with pride, showcasing their transformation from situations of distress to financial prowess. Credit champions are not immune to difficulties; what differentiates them is their ability to derive strength from vulnerabilities.

Unyielding Determination

Regardless of the current score, a champion remains resolute about reaching their financial targets. Each day offers a chance to implement strategies, paved by prior knowledge and persistence, pushing one step closer to their goal. Repaying debts doesn't occur overnight, and building credit is a marathon, not a sprint. Adopting a champions attitude allows an individual to stay the course, endlessly determined, fostering the patience that the journey demands.

Insight and Self-Reflection

The road to becoming a credit score champion is often an introspective one. This journey facilitates the application of lessons learned from past experiences, molding an attitude that continually encourages self-reflection. By inspecting past errors or successes in dealing with finances, champions deepen their understanding of their financial habits and tendencies. This insight is crucial in future decision-making processes, empowering them to make informed, beneficial financial choices confidently.

Empathy and Generosity

Possessing a champions attitude isn't solely about personal financial advancement; it's also about making a difference in the lives of others. Credit score champions recognize the importance of financial literacy and its capacity to solve financial woes. Imbued with empathy, they share their journey, challenges, and learning with others. The aim is to educate and assist others in developing their own champion mindset, fostering a cycle of knowledge-sharing that extends beyond personal benefit.

Encouraging Positivity

Amid the ups and downs of rebuilding credit health, a champion maintains an optimistic attitude. They savor small victories—a cleared debt here, an improved credit report there, knowing they're progressing. Celebrating these milestones imbues positivity and fuels motivation, serving as powerful reminders of how far they've come and the potential of where they can reach.

Continuous Learning

The world of credit scores and financial health is fluid. Laws change, lending practices evolve, and new opportunities arise. The credit score champion continually updates their knowledge. They invest time in reading financial news, attending webinars, and staying informed about advancements in relevant financial technology. The champions attitude is one of ceaseless learning, primed to adapt to financial dynamics.

2.3 Success Stories: Learning from Champions

Throughout this book, we have been discussing the journey to becoming a credit score champion. Emulating their characteristics, adopting their attitude and following their path can guide you towards significant financial growth. Let us meet some of these champions and learn from their transformative journeys as they navigated through the choppy sea of low credit scores to the serene waters of stellar credit health.

Conquering Debts: Emily's Persistence

A single mom working three jobs, Emily had a FICO score of just 470. The mounting credit card debts were hampering her dreams of providing a stable life for her son. Consumed by financial despair, Emily felt the need for an urgent recalibration of her financial life.

Her first step towards transformation began by understanding her financial situation completely. Gathering every bit of her financial data, she analyzed her credit report details, identified inaccuracies, and disputed them diligently. She used budgeting tools and apps to track spending, allowing her to identify areas where she could reduce expenses and allocate more towards debt repayments.

Feeling trapped in her high-interest credit card debts, Emily requested a meeting with her respective lenders. Bravely and humbly, she expressed her financial predicament, willingness to repay, and requested a feasible repayment plan with a lowered interest rate. To her delight, the lenders agreed. Emily was tenacious and disciplined in her repayments, ensuring she didn't miss any due dates.

Fast forward a couple of years later, Emily, now debt-free, is a beacon of financial inspiration. Her credit score stands at a brilliant 750, and she's successfully taken out a mortgage for her dream home!

Rising from Bankruptcy: David's Resilience

Life threw a curveball at David, a proud small business owner, who filed for bankruptcy following the financial devastation caused by an unforeseen disaster. Having lost his business and reeling under personal debt, his credit score was a dismal 330.

David, however, was a man with an unyielding spirit and determination. Post-bankruptcy, he came across resources that taught him about rebuilding credit. He started by opening a secured credit card account. By maintaining absolutely low utilization and ensuring timely payments, he was demonstrating responsible credit behavior, slowly rebuilding his creditworthiness from the ground up.

Parallelly, he also took a car loan. Repaying it meticulously, David was steadfast in creating a diverse credit mix contributing positively to his credit score. Within two years, his credit score had hiked to over 500. Four more years down the line, David now boasts a score of 780, proof of his financial rebuilding.

Beating the Odds: Lily's Determination

Lily, a young immigrant working at a fast-food joint, was haunted by a glaringly low credit score of 400. Despite her limited income and lack of financial knowledge, Lily was determined to overcome her economic status.

She sought help from non-profit organizations that offered free credit counseling and education. Armed with newfound financial knowledge, she opened a secured credit card, keeping utilization extremely low and paying her bills timely. Simultaneously, she also started to save consistently, however small the amount.

Dedicated to frugality, within just three years, Lily's credit score rose to a respectable 650. After another year of continued financial discipline, Lily's score crossed the 700-mark, highlighting her victorious financial journey despite overwhelming odds.

Seemingly ordinary individuals, Emily, David, and Lily have illustrious tales of becoming credit score champions. Their stories are not just inspiring, but they are also etched with lessons: a champion's mindset, the power of financial knowledge, tenacity, disciplined behavior, and the courage to face and surmount challenges are the illuminated landmarks on the path to a stellar credit score.

These stories remind us that transformations do not occur overnight. As evident in Emily's, David's, and Lily's journeys, overcoming financial adversities is a marathon of determination, resilience, and building new habits. Their narratives also resonate with the universal power of hope. No matter how crushing your current financial predicament might feel, there's a way out, a route leading to financial freedom and the sense of incomparable joy upon reaching one's goals.

2.4 Charting Your Path to Championship

Your Unique Map to Better Credit

Embarking on the journey from poor or average credit scores to becoming a credit score champion is not unlike exploring unknown territories. To navigate and arrive successfully, you need an accurate and detailed map that outlines the topography, warns of possible obstacles, and shows the most efficient route. This chapter intends to provide you with that map — tailored specifically to your unique financial landscape.

Every individual's financial journey is unique and diverse, marked with distinct challenges and victories. Hence, there can be no one-size-fits-all route towards credit score championship. Despite that, certain crucial steps — consistent across different credit situations — bolster everyone's road to a better score. Let's delve into these universal steps.

1. Acknowledge and Understand Your Financial Situation

Possibly the most difficult yet critical step to commence your journey is confronting your financial reality. This step involves more than just acknowledging that you have a low credit score or many outstanding debts. It involves understanding your financial habits, your spending patterns, and the root causes contributing to your current financial state.

To conquer mountains, one must first learn about them, their altitude, terrain, and weather patterns. Similarly, to conquer your debt mountains or credit score valleys, recognize your fiscal reality in detail. Therefore, credit report analysis is a critical step. Look out for overdue debts, high credit utilization ratio, any inaccuracies, or negative entries.

2. Plan Your Journey

Any journey begins with a plan. Considering the insights garnered from a detailed understanding of your financial landscape, formulate your credit improvement plan. This plan is analogous to the roadmap we discussed earlier. It outlines your journey from your current score to your "champion" score.

Establish a budget emphasizing debt reduction if you're swamped with debts. Prioritize high-interest debts over those with lesser rates. If inaccuracies plague your credit report, the dispute process becomes part of your plan. Your plan should also include measures to improve credit utilization, payment history and credit age —essential factors affecting your credit score.

3. Implement the Plan

Implementation is where your plan breathes life and manifests in your day-to-day financial behavior. And yet, it is where most stumble or falter. Implementing your credit improvement plan requires a mix of discipline, consistency, and determination. But remember, your plan isn't carved in stone. As you progress, reassess your plan, refining and tweaking it to adapt to any changes in your financial landscape.

4. Monitor Your Progress and Celebrate Milestones

The human spirit thrives on positivity and reward. Celebrating mini-victories on the journey can be a powerful motivator. Each time you cross off a debt from your list, your credit score takes one step closer to the championship, and that's a victory worth rewarding. The reward could be something as simple as a night out or perhaps a movie night at home.

Crucial to celebrating milestones is continuously monitoring progress. Regular credit report checks are a go-to tool for progress tracking. You start noticing the fruits of your disciplined efforts reflected in your improved credit score, lower debts, and positively updated entries.

5. Learn and Adapt

At every stage of this journey, you are learning — about your financial habits, about what strategies work for you, about your capability to confront challenges and about the resilience within you. Draw from these learnings to adapt your plan, adjust your financial habits, and devise more practical strategies. Continuous learning and adaptation are your trusted companions on this journey.

Your journey isn't over once you've hit the champion score. A champion must defend their position and that connects to the other half of the journey, maintaining an excellent credit score. Similar practices of disciplined financial behavior, regular credit checks, and adaptation extend beyond reaching your goal.

Your road to credit score championship may be fraught with difficult climbs and demanding hurdles, but remember, 'It's not about the destination, it's about the journey.' The true transformation does not lie in the number your credit score portrays, but in becoming a financially responsible individual, true to their commitments, cognizant of their limits, and conscious of their choices. The journey transforms you from being an aspirant to a champion, leading you to magnanimous victories beyond the confines of credit scores alone in your financial life.

Chapter 3:
Building the Perfect Credit Foundation: Essential Elements & Strategies

3.1 Credit Report Components: A Look Under the Hood

Imagine the first time you picked up a road map. The intricate mesh of routes sprawled across an expanse of paper, lines joining, parting, and sometimes intersecting. And somewhere in that jumble, you are expected to carve your path, working your way from point A to point B. You felt, possibly, a tinge of anxiety, but with time and familiarity, you turned that initial confusion into expertise. Guiding the wheel of your financial vehicle and journeying through the labyrinth of credit is similar.

Navigating the landscape of credit begins with understanding the structure - the components of a credit report. With knowledge and familiarity of the layout, you will not only appreciate the snapshot of your financial health presented by the report but also how each element contributes to your credit score and what measures to implement to enhance these components.

The Landscape of a Credit Report

At the heart of your financial narrative, a credit report is an in-depth, exhaustive dossier detailing your credit history – a spectrum of your debt transactions, payment behaviors, account status, and more. Compiled and curated by the credit bureaus, this report is glanced at by potential lenders, insurers, landlords, and even employers to gauge your financial reliability.

In every standard credit report, you will notice specific fundamental components that provide not just a view into your credit, but a cross-sectional layering of your financial dimensions. Such core elements serve as proxy indicators of your solvency, consistency, and repayability and, therefore, become the primary influencing factors of your credit score.

The Credit Report Components

There are several key elements present in your credit report. Here's a closer look at what they represent:

Credit Report Components
A look inside your credit report

Personal Information
- Full Name.
- Date of Birth
- Address
- Phone Number
- Employer

Credit History
Details all credit accounts opened including:
- Type of credit (credit cards, auto loans, etc.)
- Date opened
- Credit limit or loan amount
- Balance
- Payment history

Inquiries
- Lists all companies that accessed your credit report
- Shows date and type of credit check

Public Records
- Bankruptcies
- Liens
- Other legal judgments

Credit Score
- Your 3-digit credit score
- The higher the better

Understanding the sections of your credit report helps you monitor your credit health

Personal Information

Long before diving into your credit standing, the report first aids verification by furnishing your personal identification details. This includes your name, address, social security number, employment data, and date of birth. This section does not influence your credit directly but is crucial for distinguishing you from others who might share your name or similar personal details.

Credit History

The heart of your credit report—this section peels back layers to reveal your credit behavior. It outlines information about each credit account you have opened, such as type (credit card, mortgage, student loan, car loan, etc.), date of account opening, credit limit or loan amount, the account balance, and your payment history. Each entry is a beacon illuminating your repayment discipline, credit utilization, and general conduct of managing borrowed money, which contributes significantly to your credit score.

Inquiries

Every time a lender or an authorized entity initiates a check on your credit report, it's documented in the inquiries segment. Inquiries are categorized as soft and hard. Soft queries—for instance, when you check your credit report—do not impact your score. However, frequent hard inquiries—for example, when you apply for loans or credit cards—can take a toll on your credit score in the short term and convey credit desperation.

Public Records and Collections

Information such as bankruptcies, tax liens, or civil judgments against you is compiled under the public records section. Subsequently, defaulted debts handed over to collections agencies are also noted here. These entries radiate as glaring distress signals, dragging down your credit score substantially. Clearing dues and staying out of trouble are the best prevention here.

Credit Score

Lastly, reflecting the cumulative judgment of all the above is your credit score, an indicator of your creditworthiness. Higher the score, brighter your financial standing in the eyes of potential lenders.

Just like that invigorating first drive, perusing your credit report may seem intimidating initially, but rest assured, empowering yourself with each component's knowledge will bring you a step closer to mastering your financial route. As experiences teach you the rules of the road, understanding these components will allow you to manipulate the levers of your financial journey. You will discern how punctual payments enhance your credit history, or how mindful credit utilization contributes positively to the score, and more.

Imagine now, understanding your report well enough to spot errors or discrepancies, curb them at their onset, and steer clear of credit mishaps. Imagine using this component-wise knowledge to construct a sturdy credit foundation, resist the pull of quick fixes, and adopt holistic credit improvement measures. Undoubtedly, the benefits are compelling!

In graphically representing your credit, your report provides a treasure trove of information, an under-the-hood look into your financial profile. By understanding it, you reduce the chaos, simplify the wide-ranging information, articulate an action plan and translate the document into a language of credit success.

For each step in your journey, you could consider including a visual representation of your credit report. You can include infographics demonstrating each component's importance and how its function varies among different individuals. Furthermore, a side-by-side comparison illustrating positive and negative impacts on personal credit can help readers visualize the impact of their actions on their credit history. Including visuals like these could assist readers in better understanding the concept discussed in the chapter.

Always remember, understanding a credit report is not merely about figuring out what a good report looks like, but crafting it into a personal navigational tool, a financial compass guiding you along the journey of credit mastery. Take this initial step vitally, for it is the beginning of becoming a credit score champion!

3.2 Laying a Concrete Credit Foundation

Understanding the map from Chapter 3.1 is the first part of the journey; now, you hold the possibility of navigating the credit landscape. This understanding is your beacon, lighting the path towards financial prosperity. But to make the journey, you need to start preparing. And like any journey worth its weight, the expedition into credit mastery builds upon a sturdy and well-laid foundation.

The blueprint of your credit foundation lies rooted in your financial behaviors and your understanding of the essential elements of a credit report as discussed in the previous section. Now, you are equipped with the necessary tools—knowledge about personal information, credit history, inquiries, public records and collections, and your credit score. To transform this knowledge into action, let's discuss the strategies essential to laying a sound credit foundation.

Sowing the Seeds of a Robust Credit Foundation

Building a robust credit foundation commences at the roots—the core concepts you've learned so far. But like a seed, it needs to be planted in the right environment and cared for to grow. In credit terms, this nurturing comes from your financial practices.

To lay a concrete credit foundation, your first step is to establish a steady stream of income. It's the lifeline of your credit profile. A reliable income not only makes lenders view you as a credible borrower but also keeps your financial life stable. It enables you to manage your debts responsibly, meet your financial obligations, and save for future goals.

Once you have a reliable income, initiate a systematic savings plan. Nothing fortifies your credit base as effectively as a well-fed savings account. It serves as your financial backup during rainy days, an emergency buffer against unforeseen expenses that can take a toll on your credit profile when unprepared.

Simultaneously, start budgeting. Budgeting is the compass guiding your financial journey, ensuring that you steer clear from the quicksand of overspending, helping you to manage your debts effectively, and gradually building up a strong credit history.

Consider Deborah, a school teacher from Montana. Deborah struggled with a low FICO score hovering around 560 due to sporadic income, high debts, and late payments—all screaming signs of an unstable financial footing. Then she decided to make a change. She found a steady teaching job, started budgeting her monthly expenses, and made a habit of setting aside a small proportion of her income as savings. These initial steps fortified her financial base and set the foundation for her credit improvements. Within a year, her FICO score reached a respectable 700.

Building the Blocks

Once you have sown the seeds and ensured a robust base, the next steps involve building upon this base. And for that, we turn to credit accounts.

Opening a credit account is akin to putting your training into practice, to test your understanding of the credit world. A first credit account—be it a credit card, student loan, auto loan, or any form of credit—sets the ball rolling in building your credit history. It is your first formal introduction to the realm of credit and your first opportunity to demonstrate financial responsibility.

As you start using your first credit account responsibly by maintaining minimal usage and ensuring timely payments, you are laying the bricks of a strong credit foundation. Each timely payment adds a reinforcing layer to this foundation, making it sturdier, enhancing your credit history, and boosting your credit score.

For instance, let's take Kevin, an engineering student from Michigan. With no credit history, Kevin applied for and received a student credit card. He made small purchases on the card every month, consistently paid back the entire balance before the due date, and never once exceeded the 30% credit utilization rate. Within six months, Kevin's credit history reflected responsible credit usage and on-time payments, boosting his credit score from nonexistent to a solid 720.

Staying on Track

Importantly, laying a concrete credit foundation involves consistent monitoring and improvement. Regular check-ins on your credit report, recognizing mistakes, and rectifying them at the onset prevent potential cracks from widening in your credit foundation. It keeps you abreast of your credit status, allowing essential alterations or proactive measures to be implemented for continual credit improvement.

Put simply, laying a concrete credit foundation is less about scale and more about consistency. It's not about opening multiple credit accounts or making big-ticket purchases. It's about nurturing steady income, judicious budgeting, building a healthy savings buffer, managing your first credit account responsibly, and consistently monitoring your credit progress. Like any journey, it begins with a single step—a commitment to conscientious financial behavior.

As you embark on this journey, remember that every responsible decision you make translates into a better credit score, and ultimately, a healthier financial profile. Lay a mindful foundation, nurture it, monitor it, and then build upon it. This concrete credit foundation is your launchpad to financial freedom.

3.3 Fundamental Strategies for a Healthy Credit Profile

Building a healthy credit profile is not an overnight sprint; it's more akin to a marathon. By utilizing core strategies and nurturing diligent financial habits, you can secure the longevity of your credit health. This journey requires careful planning, regular reviews, alterations if necessary, and adaptability to the ever-evolving financial landscape.

Understanding Your Own Financial Health

At the heart of these strategies lies a comprehensive understanding of your own financial health. Similar to acknowledging your physical health involves a regular check-up, a deep understanding of your financial health addresses a critical and often overlooked aspect of credit profile management. This realization involves the ability to reign in your spending habits, manage your debts, and analyze your future needs and aspirations.

Embedding self-awareness into your financial life shapes you into a conscientious borrower. By aligning your financial conduct with your needs rather than your desires, you create an intrinsic framework that guides your spending, repayment, and borrowing habits.

Consider the example of Sarah, a single mother of two in California. Sarah struggled with massive credit card debts and was finding it difficult to manage her repayments. She decided to conduct a thorough analysis of her income and spending habits.

Sarah realized that a significant portion of her monthly income went towards retail therapy and dining out. It was an 'aha' moment for her to realize how these seemingly small indulgences added up to a substantial percentage of her income, creating a ripple effect on her credit health.

Recognizing the problem entailed the initial step towards regaining charge of her financial conduct. Sarah pivoted her unnecessary spending habits and focused her income towards repaying her debts, eventually carving out a smoother pathway to credit recovery.

Keeping a Low Credit Utilization Ratio

One of the key components influencing your credit score is your credit utilization ratio—the percentage of your available credit that you're using at a given time. A high utilization ratio may indicate you're overspending and might have difficulty managing your debts, potentially lowering your credit score.

Keeping this ratio low, ideally below 30%, demonstrates to lenders that you're a responsible borrower, even when the credit is available. Rather than maxing out your credit limit, consistent low credit utilization habits can fortify your credit profile and work towards enhancing your credit score over time.

Our example here is of Daniel, a salesman from Seattle, who was an aggressive credit card user. Daniel was a disciplined individual who always paid his credit card bills in full and on time. However, his heavy reliance on his credit card for every day, and often high-value, purchases demonstrated a high credit utilization ratio.

Daniel wasn't overspending or living beyond his means, but his heavy credit card usage painted a different picture to lenders, resulting in a stagnant credit score. Daniel's credit advisor suggested he keep his credit utilization ratio below 30%. Heeding this advice, Daniel started using cash or debit cards for some purchases and watched as his credit score slowly but steadily started to rise.

Diversifying Credit Mix

A well-diversified credit mix gives an edge to your credit profile. It suggests you can manage different types of credits—like student loans, auto loans, and mortgage—along with credit cards responsibly. This healthy blend of credit types can slowly strengthen your credit profile, provided they're managed wisely with regular, on-time payments.

Take, for example, Maria, a university student from Denver. As a young adult, Maria received her first credit card but wisely opted to use it sparingly, keeping her credit utilization low. During her university years, Maria took out a small student loan. Though it was a debt, it diversified the type of credit in her profile.

Maria made stringent efforts to service her student loan and credit card bill on time. Over her university lifetime, she showed responsible management of both revolving (from her credit card) and installment credits (from her student loan). This responsible mixed credit use placed her in good credit standing, boosting her credit score.

Regular Credit Report Checks
Regular credit report checks form the backbone of these strategies, enabling you to understand your current credit standing and rectify errors promptly. Discrepancies or fraudulent activities can often slip into your credit report, affecting your credit score. Routine checks can help identify these early, preventing potential damage to your credit profile.

Amy, a software engineer from New York, understood this well when she detected fraudulent activity during one of her routine credit report checks. She acted swiftly, contacting her financial institution and disputing the fraudulent transaction immediately, preventing further damage to her credit score.

A healthy credit profile is not a destination but an ongoing journey. It's one where self-awareness, keeping a low credit utilization ratio, diversifying your credit mix, and performing regular credit report checks act as travel companions, guiding you and ensuring your journey is on a smooth trajectory.

3.4 Avoiding Pitfalls: Dodging Negative Entries

Embarking on the journey to perfect credit isn't simply about building an admirable credit profile; it's equally about sidestepping potential missteps that could trip you up along the way. Negative entries on your credit report, such as late payments, defaults, bankruptcies, or collections, can cast a long, unfavorable shadow on your credit profile, marring your reputation in the eyes of potential lenders. In this chapter, we dive into the strategies for nimbly avoiding these pitfalls, which, if neglected, can cause a severe detriment to your credit health.

Being Proactive: The Power of Timely Payments

Possessing credit isn't just about establishing financial history; it's an ongoing commitment to maintain responsible financial behavior— most crucially, making timely repayments. Delinquent payments are a glaring red flag to lenders, subtly revealing fiscal irresponsibility and the potential for further risk. A single late payment may seem harmless in the grand scheme of your financial journey, but, if recurrent, can pile on to significantly dent your credit score and confidence of the lenders.

Consider Helen's journey. A diligent worker, Helen's meticulous nature extended to her financial habits, making it a point to pay her bills in full and on time. A sudden medical emergency, however, threw her off track as she struggled to juggle her medical bills along with her other financial obligations. Missed deadlines led to a delinquent payment appearing on her credit report, surprisingly lowering her hitherto robust credit score.

Frustrated and worried, Helen decided to take charge of her finances and created an action plan. She ensured she prioritized her bill repayments, organized reminders to prevent any future missed payments, and even created an emergency fund to cover unexpected expenses. Improved fiscal management led to her eventually regaining her credit score peak and maintaining it, demonstrating that circumventing pitfalls required not merely immediate action but continued vigilance in managing personal finances.

Steering Clear Of High Debt

While credit enables financial opportunities, it's easy to lapse into a trap of excessive spending and accruing high-level debt. Credit, in reality, equates to borrowed money. Borrowing more than you can afford to repay leads to an increase in your credit utilization ratio, negatively impacting your credit score. In essence, it's a financial quicksand from which recovery can be tediously slow, arduous, and damaging to your credit health.

Pete, a business owner from Texas, hit a gold vein with his venture. Accustomed to his newly acquired wealth, he splashed out on luxury purchases with his credit card, confident in his ability to repay his accruing debt. An unexpected downfall in his business, however, led to financial instability, and his accruing debt proportional to his extravagant purchases began to pile up.

His high debt and inability to manage repayments led to sustained damage to his credit score. Struggling, he decided to tackle his financial turmoil head-on. Pete adopted stringent austerity measures, curbing his extraneous purchases. He also availed a debt management plan to effectively handle his financial obligations, committing to a fixed monthly budget and implementing a strict repayment strategy. Gradually, he managed to regain control over his financial life and slowly claw his way back from the brink, illustrating the necessity of avoiding the pitfall of unnecessary debt to maintain credit health.

Dodging Bankruptcy Like A Plague

Bankruptcy is the financial equivalent of a nuclear disaster. It's a last-resort measure that, while providing temporary respite from unmanageable debt, leaves long-term scars on your credit profile. It dramatically reduces your credit score and stays on your credit history for seven to ten years, acting as a deterrent for potential lenders.

Robert, a car dealer from Michigan, painfully learned this reality when a series of unfortunate events shook his stable financial world upside down. Deep in debt and struggling to keep his business afloat, he filed for Chapter 7 bankruptcy, aiming to wipe out his debts.

Though this action did temporarily relieve his immediate financial pressure, it drastically reduced his credit score and hampered his chances of securing credit for the subsequent years. Over time, Robert worked hard to rebuild his credit, making very strategic decisions, keeping his spending in check, and making consistent on-time repayments. He successfully managed to rebuild his credit profile, but it was an uphill battle, stressing the need to regard bankruptcy as a last resort measure, not a quick solution.

Staying vigilant to avoid the pitfalls of late payments, avoiding high debt, and dodging bankruptcy demands an acute awareness of your financial habits and recognising the early warning signs of potential dangers. Developing different plans for different financial needs, maintaining an emergency fund, and avoiding excessive debt can enable you to successfully dodge these damaging entries and boost your credit profile's overall health.

Chapter 4:

The Dark Side of Lending: Identifying Unethical Practices

4.1 Understanding Predatory Lending

Spotting the Sharks: What is Predatory Lending?

Spotting a shark in a sea of benign sea creatures can be a tranquilizing thought - imagine being able to avoid a financial predator before they cause damage. This is the essence of understanding predatory lending. Predatory lending is an abusive practice conducted by unscrupulous lenders who prey on unsuspecting borrowers through manipulative sales tactics, deceptive loan terms, and exorbitant interest rates. It's akin to swimming with sharks, where the predatory lenders are the sharks, the unsuspecting victims are the ordinary fishes, and the sea is the vast landscape of the lending market.

Now, why should understanding predatory lending matter to you? It's simple. Awareness is your best defense. As someone striving to enhance your credit or maintain a good credit rating, it's of utmost importance to steer clear of these dangerous lending approaches that can impose devastating financial consequences.

The Anatomy of Predatory Lending: Tactics, Traits, and Techniques

Predatory lending practices manifest in various forms. They could include hidden fees layered into loan agreements, loan flipping where borrowers are coerced into refinancing multiple times, equity stripping involving consequential default due to excessive borrowing, or balloon payments where borrowers are helpless under the weight of large final payments.

Understanding predatory lending involves gaining familiarity with fraudulent techniques used by these loan sharks. They often exploit the borrower's lack of understanding or desperation for urgent funds, applying pressure tactics to coax borrowers into unfavorable loan terms. Some predatory lenders specifically target vulnerable populations such as senior citizens, low-income individuals, single parents, or immigrants with limited English proficiency - those they believe lack credit alternatives or the knowledge to perceive their deceit.

Owing to the idiosyncrasies of predatory lending, it becomes vital for potential borrowers to recognize the markers. Loan terms that are extensively complicated, lenders appearing overly aggressive or not disclosing all terms and fees upfront, are some of the many warning signs.

Impact of Predatory Lending: Financial Peril and Credit Turmoil

Behind the veneer of immediate funds or fast approvals which predatory lenders often use to entice borrowers, lurk far-reaching repercussions. Individuals ensnared by such loans are liable to sink into the quagmire of debts, which could lead to serious financial strain or even bankruptcy.

The toxic fallout of predatory lending does not stop at strained bank accounts or depleted savings. They further translate into a long-lasting, detrimental impact on credit scores. Defaulting or falling behind on predatory loan repayments not only plummet your credit score but leaves a negative stain on your credit report that might take years to rectify. This blemished record could cause future lenders to perceive you as a high-risk borrower, which could result in being denied credit, or approved only at significantly higher interest rates.

The Haven in Legitimate Lending: Fighting Back

Contrary to predatory lending, an ethical lending approach focuses on the borrower's ability to repay the loan without causing extreme financial distress. Legitimate lenders practise full transparency, providing information about the cost and terms of loans upfront, and treating borrowers fairly regardless of their credit background.

In our fight against predatory lending, two words stand tall — knowledge and vigilance. Only when you understand the nefarious tactics employed and remain alert to potential traps, can you safeguard yourself against these predatory practices. It's all in the mindset; adopting a financially disciplined and informed approach is key to swerving away from the path that leads to financial equivocation.

If you find yourself encountering a potential predatory lender, remember that you, as a consumer, have rights and protections. Reach out to local consumer protection agencies, report the unfair practices, seek help from credit counselors, or take legal action if necessary.

Concluding Thoughts

Understanding predatory lending involves recognizing the manipulation and deceit inherent in these unfair lending practices. It is about standing as a bulwark against financial exploitation and credit turmoil. By educating yourself about predatory lending patterns, tactics and repercussions, you equip yourself with the ammunition to fight back.

Resilience and prevention are the mantras. Stay proactive, stay informed, and stay steadfast in your resolve to maintain the hard-earned credit foundation you are building. Remember, your financial independence stands testament not just to your past fiscal discipline, but also to your present-day perseverance in safeguarding your credit against predatory perils.

4.2: The True Cost of Payday Loans – More Than What Meets the Eye

A Tempting Solution or a Financial Pitfall?

Imagine this: It's the middle of the month and a sudden car breakdown, unexpected medical bill, or any unforeseen expense comes up. You have a whole two weeks before your next paycheck arrives. Panicking, you see an advertisement for a payday loan – fast, easy money to tide you over. Tempting, isn't it?

Payday loans are a type of short-term, high-interest loan that can seem like a quick and easy solution to those caught in a financial crunch. Often, they require little more than proof of income and a checking account to qualify. But that's exactly where the fairytale ends and the nightmare begins.

The Price Tag Behind Payday Loans – The 'Interest-ing' Tale

At first glance, payday loans might appear not that costly. A charge of $15 to borrow $100 seems pretty reasonable. However, tally it up to an annual rate, and you'll see an entirely different picture. That 15% charge for a two-week loan translates to an annual percentage rate (APR) of almost 400%!

To throw light on it, consider this. If you go towards traditional lending routes – personal loans, credit cards – the APRs typically range between 12-30%. Would you willingly buy a product or service that costs over 10 times more than its original price? Probably not, unless it was a dire emergency, and herein lies the prime allure and the danger of payday loans.

The Debt Trap – Rolling Over the Loans

Here's where it gets even murkier. The structure of payday loans often leads borrowers into a trap of debt. Most people who take out payday loans are unable to pay them back in 14 days. So, they "roll over" the loan— taking another payday loan to pay off the first one. This leads to a vicious circle of rollovers. Each time this happens, the cost of the loan increases with new interest charges, trapping the borrower in a cycle of growing and inescapable debt.

To sketch an example, assume that you took out a $400 payday loan with a fee of $60. By the time your next paycheck comes in, other expenses come knocking on the door, making it impossible for you to pay off the initial loan. You decide to roll over the loan. Now, you owe $460 ($400 plus a new fee of $60). If you continue to roll the loan over a couple of more times, the fees alone could exceed the initial loan amount.

Weighing the Emotional Cost – The Stress That Follows Suit

The cost of payday loans isn't just monetary; it also includes severe emotional and mental strain. The relentless pressure of accumulating debt, combined with the uncertainty of getting out of the vicious cycle, can lead to sleepless nights and anxiety. The immediate relief provided at the start quickly morphs into stress, fear and a constant state of financial unrest.

Spurring the Community Economy – Or Perhaps Not?

Some argue that payday lenders contribute to local economies by serving an overlooked market segment. While it's true they provide funds to individuals who might struggle to obtain funding otherwise, it's important to consider the long-term implications. A community populated with individuals entrapped in payday loan debt is unlikely to prosper. A large portion of people's income would go into servicing high-interest loans, leaving less money for spending or saving. Not the most promising scenario for a thriving economic setting, is it?

Wrapping It All Up

In a nutshell, payday loans constitute a risky and costly financial solution that could prove significantly more expensive than most borrowers realize at the outset. They might promise fast and easy money, but the real cost comes in the form of outrageously high APRs, the risk of falling into a cycle of debt, severe emotional strain, and potentially detrimental effects on local economies.

As a person striving to push your credit score up the ladder, it's important to understand the true cost of payday loans and explore other alternatives. Instead of reaching for a quick fix that potentially turns into a long-term problem, consider seeking assistance from a credit counselor, devising a budget, or exploring low-interest rate borrowing alternatives as a proactive step towards maintaining your financial health.

4.3 Spotting Loan Scams – A Stitch in Time Saves Nine

In an ideal world, everyone looking to borrow money would have access to fair, transparent, and above board lending practices. Unfortunately, we are far from that ideal world. Scores of hard-working individuals and hopeful homeowners frequently fall prey to the snares of illegitimate lenders, losing not just their money, but also their peace of mind in scams artfully designed to exploit their urgent need for loan assistance. This chapter aims to be your guiding light through this murky territory, helping you identify, sidestep, and report loan scams.

The Wide, Wild World of Loan Scams

The onus is on us to be vigilant, as loan fraudsters are adept at manipulating the parameters of trust. These scams generally first appear as a glimmer of hope in the borrower's life, promising to solve their immediate financial constraints. Instead, the unwitting borrower falls into a quicksand trap, drawing them deeper into a financial abyss. The scam artists use varied tactics to deceive borrowers and can range from advanced fee fraud, loan flipping, to the more pernicious debt collection scams.

Let's dig a little deeper into these categories to understand how they operate:

Advanced fee fraud: In these scams, borrowers are told they've qualified for a very attractive loan but must pay a fee, generally a percentage of the loan's total, before receiving the loan proceeds. These initial fees are often hefty and, once paid, the promised loan never materializes while the scam artist disappears with the fee.

Loan flipping: This is a common scam in the mortgage loan sector. Here, predatory lenders entice borrowers with better loan terms, lower monthly payments, or a cash-out refinance. However, these offers often come with hidden fees and charges, and before the borrower realizes, they are trapped in a cycle of refinancing that never benefits them but continues to enrich the scam lender.

Debt collection scams: In these hoaxes, fraudsters pose as debt collectors and intimidate or threaten borrowers into paying debts they don't even owe. It's a fear tactic that capitalizes on the borrower's lack of knowledge about their rights and the collection process.

Signs You're Being Scammed – The Red Flags

Knowing what to look for is the key to avoiding loan scams. There are some distinct signs that scream 'scam,' and being able to identify these can save you from significant financial and emotional distress.

Advance fee requirement: Reputable lenders do not ask for fees upfront before a loan is approved. If you're asked to pay a fee to 'secure' your loan, it's a bright red flag signaling a scam.

Guaranteed approval: Guaranteed approval does not exist in the lending world. If a lender assures you of a loan without inspecting your credit report or asking for personal financial information, it's a telltale sign of a potential scam.

Unregistered lenders: Any legitimate lender should be registered in the state where they operate. If you cannot find any licensing information about the lender, be sure to double-check their authenticity before proceeding.

High-pressure sales tactics: Genuine lenders do not push or rush you into accepting loan offers. Predatory lenders, however, frequently resort to pressuring tactics, urging you to act fast, or pushing for a quick sign-up.

Unconventional communication channels: If your lender is inordinately fond of communication through non-official channels, like personal mobile numbers or messaging apps, it should be cause for concern.

Vague or unclear loan terms: Legitimate lenders always provide detail about the loan terms, rates, and penalties. If you encounter ambiguous or unclear loan terms, it's akin to courting danger.

Outsmarting Scammers – The Triple-R Strategy

If you suspect you've encountered a loan scam, it is vital to respond promptly, and the actions to take can be distilled into a simple Triple-R strategy: Recognize, Report, and Recover.

Recognize: The first step in tackling a scam is by acknowledging that you have fallen for one. There is no shame in it; even the most seasoned individuals can be duped by skilled fraudsters.

Report: Reporting the scam to your state's consumer protection office, the Federal Trade Commission, or the Financial and Fraud Enforcement Task Force can help prevent others from getting scammed and enable law enforcement to cut the supply line to these fraudsters.

Recover: Consulting with a professional counselor and working on rebuilding your personal finance will help you move towards recovery quickly.

Arming yourself with the right knowledge can make you impervious to the tactics of loan scammers. An informed borrower is a safe borrower, and by learning to spot loan scams, equipping yourself with the ability to respond, and knowing where I how to report these frauds, you can ensure your financial stability is never compromised.

4.4 Your Rights as a Borrower

The ability to borrow money is a powerful tool. It gives you the opportunity to make significant purchases, invest in your future, and manage unexpected expenses. However, just as a sharp knife can help you in the kitchen but harm you if used carelessly, borrowing money should be handled judiciously and responsibly. Ensuring success in your financial journey extends beyond just understanding credit scores, managing loans and credit cards wisely, or even avoiding scams. It requires a comprehensive knowledge of your rights as a borrower. Understanding these rights will arm you with the confidence to deal with lenders, solve disputes, and demand fair treatment.

Right to a Transparent and Fair Lending Process

A cornerstone in borrower rights is the right to a transparent and fair lending process. This implies, as a borrower, you have the right to know all the terms and conditions associated with the loan, including details about the interest rate, additional fees, the payment schedule, and the total costs over the loan's lifetime. Lenders must present this information clearly, not buried in fine print or shrouded in ambiguous language.

Right to Equal Opportunity in Lending

Your right as a borrower also encapsulates the right to equal opportunity in lending. The Equal Credit Opportunity Act (ECOA) prohibits lenders from discriminating against borrowers based on factors like race, color, religion, national origin, sex, marital status, age, or receipt of income from any public assistance program. If you've ever faced discrimination in your loan application process, remember this act empowers you with the right to file a complaint against the lender.

Right to Privacy of Information

Privacy is another facet of your rights that needs careful attention. A lender may need certain personal and financial data from you to evaluate your loan application, but that doesn't give them free rein over your information. Remember, you have the right to know why the lender needs the information, how they will use it, and who they might share it with. You also have the right to ensure your information is kept confidential and not used for unwanted promotional or marketing purposes.

Right to Fair Collections Practices

Should there be an unfortunate situation where you can't keep up with your loan payments, remember your rights still protect you. The Fair Debt Collection Practices Act (FDCPA) obliges lenders and debt collectors to treat you fairly and prohibits them from using deceptive or abusive practices to collect money from you. They can't harass you with constant phone calls, make false statements, or use unfair ways to collect the debt. You also have the right to dispute the debt, request information about the debt's origination, and even ask the debt collector to stop contacting you.

Let's consider John's case as an illustrative example. John, a diligent worker, was laid off during the pandemic and could no longer meet his loan repayment schedule. He was already under financial stress when the constant harassing calls from the debt collector started, causing him added anxiety. However, John was aware of his rights as a borrower. He wrote a letter to the debt collector citing the FDCPA and asking them to cease contact. This simple act, empowered by his knowledge of his rights, brought him immediate relief from the harassment.

Right to Complain and Seek Redress

Amid your financial journey, if you ever feel your rights are being infringed upon, remember that you have the right to voice your complaint and seek resolution. Regulated lenders and financial institutions have complaint management systems in place, and you have every right to utilize those systems. You also have the right to approach regulatory authorities like the Consumer Financial Protection Bureau or your state consumer protection office if you think your complaint isn't being addressed satisfactorily by the lender.

Just like how Thomas, a homeowner, did when he found his lender was charging him dubious fees. Thomas tried resolving the dispute with the lender first, but when he found them dismissive of his concerns, he did not back down. He filed a complaint with the state consumer protection office. His knowledge of his rights as a borrower allowed him to rectify the situation and avoid paying unfair charges.

These rights empower you as a borrower, serving as your shield in the battlefield of credit and lending, enabling you to demand fair treatment, and exercise concern over your financial matters confidently. Remember, it is your responsibility to be aware of these rights, invoke them when necessary, and take action if they are violated. Your financial journey is one of empowerment and control, and understanding your rights as a borrower is fundamental towards that journey.

Chapter 5:

Credit Karma Unlocked: The Secret Algorithm Behind FICO Scoring

5.1 Demystifying the FICO Score Algorithm

The FICO score algorithm, an essential component in consumer credit, plays a critical role in determining the creditworthiness of millions of Americans. By grasping the intricacies of this algorithm, we can achieve not only a better understanding of our financial standing but also take control of our credit narrative.

The Science Behind the FICO Score Algorithm

Fair Isaac Corporation (FICO) developed its eponymous scoring model in 1989 to standardize the assessment of individuals' credit risk. The FICO score, ranging from 300 (lowest) to 850 (highest), weighs various factors of your credit history and behavior to produce an accurate measure of your creditworthiness. Lenders, banks, and other financial institutions rely on your FICO score to gauge your ability to repay loans and the likelihood of default.

Understanding the pillars of the FICO score algorithm empowers you to develop a well-rounded credit profile. FICO organizes these pillars into five core components:

- **Payment History (35%):** Your record of timely bill payments forms a foundation for a solid credit score. Late or missed payments significantly impact your creditworthiness and, consequently, your FICO score. To excel in this sector, focus on consistent, punctual bill payments.
- **Amounts Owed (30%):** Also known as "credit utilization," this refers to the portion of your credit limit currently being used. It takes into account balances on all your credit accounts. A lower credit utilization rate reflects healthy credit usage, which favorably influences your FICO score. Experts recommend keeping credit utilization below 30%.
- **Length of Credit History (15%):** This factor measures the age of your oldest and newest credit accounts, as well as the average age of all accounts. The longer you have responsibly managed credit, the stronger this component of your FICO score.

- **Credit Mix (10%):** A diverse blend of credit types—such as mortgages, student loans, credit cards, and auto loans—reflects financial adaptability and responsibility, positively impacting your FICO score. However, avoid obtaining new credit accounts solely to improve this factor.
- **New Credit (10%):** FICO considers new credit inquiries, recently opened accounts, and the time since the opening of these accounts while evaluating your credit risk. Avoid applying for multiple credit lines within a short period, as each application incurs a hard inquiry and may negatively impact your score.

Decoding the Credit Score Range

The FICO score range can be broken down into several brackets, correlating to different credit risk levels:

Being aware of your FICO score and where you stand in the scale empowers you to target areas for improvement, ultimately boosting both your creditworthiness and your score.

Your Score and Continuous Improvement

It's essential to acknowledge that the FICO score algorithm is continually evolving, adapting to changing patterns in consumer behavior and credit risk assessment. Additionally, the algorithm is sensitive to fluctuations in your credit profile. As a result, your credit score requires constant maintenance to ensures its upward trajectory.

Monitoring your FICO score and credit report for inaccuracies or irregularities is critical. Should you find an erroneous or outdated negative entry, take the necessary steps to dispute the information and have it removed. The marriage of vigilance and active credit management will guide you towards credit score success.

In conclusion, demystifying the FICO score algorithm is the first step to seizing control of your credit destiny. By understanding the factors the algorithm considers, you can shape your financial behavior to enhance your credit profile and attain higher FICO scores. Ensure regular monitoring, dispute incorrect information, and maintain your financial discipline to ascend the FICO score ladder, unlocking new opportunities and achieving financial freedom.

5.2 The Science of Credit Karma

Credit Karma has invariably emerged as a dependable, consumer-friendly tool in the world of credit scores. Born out of an aspiration to demystify credit for everyday individuals, it has grown into a one-stop platform that not only provides free credit reports but also unravels the complexity wrapped around credit scores. But, how does it work? What's the science behind Credit Karma's genius? Isn't it fascinating that it mirrors and informs us of the exact FICO scores used by banks, car lenders, and credit card companies, free of cost?

The Inception: Understanding Credit Karma

Credit Karma's existence took root in the grain of technology when three pioneers saw a need to democratize financial information. The goal was clear - make credit and loan management accessible and easy to understand for the general public. Credit Karma served to empower individuals, giving them the necessary tools to take control of their financial destinies.

The Free Access Philosophy: How does Credit Karma make profit?
While most companies might charge for credit score access, Credit Karma adheres to the philosophy of free access. The question that arises is - how does Credit Karma generate revenue? This is where targeted advertising for financial products comes into play. Whenever a user applies for a credit card or a loan through a promotion on their platform, Credit Karma receives a commission. This model gives them the ability to provide an array of services to users for free.

The Credit Karma Scoring Model: VantageScore 3.0

Unlike most traditional models, which use the FICO scoring model, Credit Karma uses the VantageScore 3.0 model, formulated by the three major credit bureaus: Experian, Equifax, and TransUnion. With a score range of 300 to 850, VantageScore allocates consumers into similar brackets as FICO. The spectrum categorizes them from poor credit risk to exceptional credit risk.

The factors considered by the VantageScore model resemble those of FICO. It studies your payment history, credit utilization ratio, length of credit history, and more to determine a score. The weightage, however, varies from that of FICO. For instance, VantageScore places a substantial emphasis on the last two years of a consumer's credit history.

Bringing Users Closer to their Financial Dreams

Credit Karma represents a leap for consumers, offering them an easy-to-navigate platform to understand their credit scores. By merely entering some basic information, the user is granted access to their credit scores, credit reports, and a personal dashboard.

The dashboard is a game-changer as it provides a complex analysis of your credit score in a simplified manner. It highlights key factors affecting the score, potential weak spots, and even provides personalized tips on improving creditworthiness.

Credit Karma goes further by providing a credit simulator. With this tool, users can visualize the potential effects of their financial behaviors. For example, it can show how much your score might decrease if you miss a payment or how it might improve if you lower your credit utilization - a proactive method for cultivating better financial habits.

Reiterating the Importance of Vigilance

While Credit Karma is an outstanding tool, it doesn't eradicate the necessity for vigilant financial management. While it provides credit scores and reports, it isn't a substitute for diligently checking your credit reports. Always supplement its use by verifying details from credit reports received directly from the bureaus.

In Conclusion

Credit Karma breaks down the burgeoning complexity of personal finance into digestible segments. It adopts a riches-to-rags approach, making peak-level credit and financial expertise accessible to anyone with an Internet connection. You can almost visualize its algorithm, tirelessly working behind the scenes to untangle webs of financial data and provide insights, making the path of financial recovery less daunting for every hopeful homeowner, struggling parent, or ambitious student.

But remember, the rise upwards is not a one-time climb. It requires consistent nurturing, monitoring, and adjusting of your financial habits. And while Credit Karma provides the tools, the onus of ascending remains on you. Hence, nurture a relationship with your credit score, treat it as a lifelong companion, and continuously strive to maintain its health for a sound financial future.

5.3 Utilizing Technology to Boost your Score

In this digital-dominated era, new-age tools and sophisticated technology have reshaped the landscape of almost every industry. Financial management and credit score improvement are no exceptions. Dedication to improving your credit score combined with smart usage of technology tools can propel your journey towards financial supremacy.

The Dawn of Digital in the Credit World

The era of traditional, paperwork-laden financial management has passed. Technology has ushered in a wave of innovation that simplifies and accelerates the journey to improve your credit score. Credit cards, bank loans, mortgages are all just clicks away, and equally convenient are measures to help handle your credit and strengthen your financial health. It's a new dawn, a time to embrace technology.

The Power of Credit Management Apps

Consider the power of credit management apps. These platforms, often free to use, can be a guiding beacon, helping you stay in control and understand the nuances of your credit journey. For instance, many credit management apps offer real-time credit score updates, allowing you to monitor your progress closely. They provide in-depth breakdowns of your scores, enlightening you about the exact elements influencing them.

A prime example is 'Mint,' an application that not only tracks your credit score in real time but simultaneously assists you with budgeting and investing. Suppose you are prone to overspending, forgetting due payments, or grappling with debt. In that case, these apps are your digital companions, ensuring you stay on track with notifications, reminders, and tools for better financial habits.

Financial Automation: A Friend or Foe?

Financial Automation is another tech-driven solution to bolstering your credit score. Automatic bill payments, for instance, can ensure you never miss a deadline, preventing late fees and possible credit score dips. Setting up autopay feature for mortgage loans or student loans can yield a consistent, flawless payment history, a significant factor influencing credit scores. Robo-advisors can lead you through investment decisions, helping you grow wealth and eventually contribute to your creditworthiness.

However, like every tool, automation must be handled wisely. Automation should not encourage ignorance towards transaction details. Always know where your money is going and why — ensure it aligns with your financial plans. This cautious approach will ensure automation remains a friend, not a foe, in your credit management journey.

Technological Support for Debt Management

For those struggling with the heavy burden of debt, a set of specialized tools brings relief. Be it credit card debt, student loans, or mortgages, technology can help formulate efficient strategies to tackle these setbacks. Debt repayment planner applications like 'Unbury.Me' generate customized payment strategies, either by the Avalanche (highest-interest-first) or Snowball (smallest-debts-first) approach. Likewise, consolidation tools can help you simulate scenarios if you're considering an amalgamation of loans. Tile, track, and eliminate, these tech tools simplify debt management significantly, thereby indirectly boosting your credit scores.

Augmenting Financial Literacy

Tools aimed at financial education further reinforce your efforts to ace the credit game. They demystify complex financial concepts, helping you comprehend what you're working with. With higher financial literacy, adopting more effective credit improvement strategies becomes easier.

Consider 'CreditWise' from Capital One. Beyond score-checking, this tool provides simulations showing how different actions can change your score, assisting you in understanding credit implications better and learning to make smarter financial decisions.

Get Your Free Annual Credit Report, Digitally

Don't forget your right to a free credit report annually from the three major credit bureaus. Websites like AnnualCreditReport.com are government-authorized sources where you can request these reports. Regular checks keep you aware of your standing and help catch inaccuracies that might harm your score, if not rectified.

In Conclusion

While technology provides a plethora of tools to manage your credit, the power to harness these lies within your hands. Remember, technology is a support system, not a substitute, for sound financial behavior. Regular checks, responsible spending, and disciplined debt repayment will always remain the foundational steps in the path to improved credit.

The wealth of financial technology simplifies and streamlines the path to improved credit scores. Still, no degree of digital innovation can replace financial discipline, vigilance, and a keen drive for continuous learning. So, wield these tools wisely, allow them to guide your journey, but remember that the onus of fruition lies on your shoulders.

5.4: The Role of AI in Credit Scoring

An Unfamiliar Player Enters the Field

As Alfred Hitchcock once said, "In many of the films now being made, there is very little cinema." An ostensibly cryptic message, yet upon parsing, Mr. Hitchcock's statement hints at the expanding presence of technology in our daily lives. A domain intrinsically linked to this phenomenon is the realm of credit scores, where one such intriguing entrant is the science of artificial intelligence or AI.

How AI Leaves an Impact

Artificial intelligence is a robust tool that has the potential to revolutionize virtually any domain of our lives, including the quite distinctive vehicle of credit scoring. Challenging established norms amidst the digits and decimals, AI, or artificial intelligence, infuses a potent driver to rev up FICO scores into unchartered territories.

AI, in essence, is all about mimicry -- mirroring human-like intelligence and capabilities. To speak colloquially, think of AI as a high-performance, ultra-dependable assistant focused on executing the game plan of credit score enhancement to perfection.

Two Ways That AI Transforms the Credit Scoring Landscape

So how does this fancy-sounding tech disrupt a realm as complex and nuanced as FICO Scoring? That happens primarily through two ways: precision prediction and holistic credit analysis.

Precision Prediction

The credit industry has long been renowned for its propensity for precision. AI takes this innate focus and dials it up to eleven. Imagine this: AI and machine learning algorithms analyze mountains of credit data, identifying patterns and trends that elude human cognition.

These algorithms analyze your past behaviors, understanding not just your current situation, but how you've evolved and are likely to continue evolving. It paints a vivid picture of your financial trajectory, providing lenders with a detailed look at your reliability as a potential borrower, which in turn guides your FICO scores.

These hyper-accurate forecasts offer a certain stark clarity, an intricate mosaic of millions, even billions of pieces, challenging aspects once purely in the hands of the mystical FICO scoring model.

Holistic Credit Analysis

One area in which AI truly flexes its muscle is its ability to conduct comprehensive, "holistic" credit analysis. Unlike conventional credit rating frameworks that often prioritize black-and-white data like payment history and credit utilization, AI translates shades of gray into discernable insights, thereby optimizing credit scoring strategies.

While traditional factors are by no means thrown into oblivious oblivion, AI takes into account data points that were previously brushed aside: events that deemed insignificant by conventional analytics but speak volumes about a potential borrower's behavior. These may include online purchase habits, regularity in utility bill payments or even digital footprint on social media platforms.

By casting a wider net, AI unearths a richer, more nuanced analysis - a more complete profile of a borrower. This expanded perspective is invaluable in the colossal task of predicting financial behavior, ultimately leading to a more accurate portrait of creditworthiness.

Accepting the Role of AI in Our Lives

Life, as author Paulo Coelho once wrote, "is a constant evolution." As evident as this statement is, it also holds true for our understanding and application of credit scores. While conventional credit scoring methods continue to hold center stage, it's this unseen conductor orchestrating unforeseen developments in the background - AI - that promises to radically shape the concert of our credit futures.

In the intriguing dance of credit scores that often left us breathless and confounded, we now find in AI a dance partner who mirrors our beats and rhythm. A partner who not only echoes our credit aspirations but goes a step beyond to partner, guide and insulate in our quest for credit elevation.

AI has already started making its mark in the world of credit scoring, and its influence is only bound to grow in extent, reach, and complexity. However, it is not to be feared or shunned, but embraced as an evolution in the field of credit. For, like dance, wrestling with the hands of destiny, it's in the harmonious blending of rhythm, routine, and innovation that memorable performances are born.

Chapter 6:
Your Ultimate 609 Dispute Letter Handbook: Proven Templates for Success

6.1 Understanding 609 Letters

Empowering Your Credit Repair Journey

Peeling away layers of complexities and misconceptions surrounding credit scores and financial credibility, we've arrived at the gateway to an invaluable tool in the credit repair arsenal — 609 Dispute Letters. Standing firmly at the confluence of legality and financial acumen, these letters are often underutilized weapons that become a beacon of hope for many caught in the entanglement of an erroneous credit report.

Unraveling the 609 Enigma

The "609" in a 609 Dispute Letter refers to Section 609 of the Fair Credit Reporting Act (FCRA), under which it finds its legal standing. This statute, designed to promote accuracy, fairness, and privacy of information within credit reporting agencies, allows consumers to request the disclosure of all the information in their credit files from the credit bureaus and seek verification of data deemed inaccurate.

The 609 letters serve a dual purpose. First, it empowers consumers to take control of their financial narratives, by meticulously screening for and combating credit report errors. Second, it opens up a dialogue with credit bureaus, engaging them in a professional quest for data verification and potential rectification.

Beyond the Plain Sight: The True Power of a 609 Letter

While on its surface, the power vested within 609 letters seems straightforward, it's the subtler implications that truly enhance its significance. With a 609 Dispute Letter, you are no longer a passive bystander in the credit scoring journey, but an active participant, orchestrating essential improvements to your score.

Consider for a moment John, a lifelong musician who attends financial chords with the same precision as his musical ones. Despite managing his payments on time and maintaining stable financial habits, John notices a sudden dip in his credit score. Unfamiliar entries on his credit report baffle him. It's here that a 609 letter becomes John's lifeline. By leveraging his right under Section 609, John effectively communicates with the credit bureau, pinpoints the errors, thus initiating their review and eventual removal.

This example underscores that information errors can appear on anyone's credit report, irrespective of their fiscal diligence. Herein lies the essence of a 609 Dispute Letter – it equips you with the power to rectify errors, thereby securing your journey towards financial stability.

Dealing with the Chiaroscuro: Shadows amid the Light

Yet, as we navigate the 609 Dispute journey, it's crucial to acknowledge the shadow to this light. A 609 dispute letter doesn't offer an easy way out of valid debts. Nor is it a guarantee to have each disputed item removed. It aids in highlighting potential mistakes but offers no magic eraser for authentic credit errors.

What it does offer, though, is an avenue of hope to correct inadvertent errors, a chance to reclaim some control over your credit score narrative. It's a torchshine upon the winding road of credit repair, which, while not eliminating all obstacles, significantly illuminates the path.

Embracing the Power of Knowledge and Initiative

As we conclude the journey through understanding 609 dispute letters, it's evident that these are more than just a drafted appeal aimed at credit repair. In essence, they champion the primal ethos of individual empowerment and self-advocacy. 609 letters embolden us to leave no stone unturned when it comes to our financial health, to actively seek precision and rectitude in our credit reports.

Exploring this realm beyond mere surface-level comprehension, you'll find that 609 Letters hold within them the ability to clear false shadows cast upon your financial credibility. For many, they signify a chance to rectify errors that could potentially disrupt dreams of owning a house or starting a business. For others, it's an opportunity to reduce the burden of abnormally high-interest rates that handcuff them to an unending cycle of debt repayment.

Through this understanding, it is evident that taking control of your financial destiny begins with a single step — grappling with the extraordinary force of the 609 dispute process that's right there at your fingertips. Embrace it, hone it, and let it serve as a catapult propelling you toward a future of solid credit and financial prosperity.

6.2 Crafting the Perfect Dispute Letter

Credit repair might seem like an uphill task, especially when inaccuracies embed themselves within your credit reports, chipping away at your hard-earned scores. Among the array of tools to combat and contest those inaccuracies, the 609 Dispute Letter holds a significant place, offering its wielder a potent remedy in the quest for credit score restoration.

In this chapter, we will provide you with absolution - a well-rounded understanding of how to construct your battle armor in the form of a 609 dispute letter, emerging stronger and ready to combat the inaccuracies that tarnish your credit portrait. We present you with tried-and-tested templates, lovingly designed and perfected through years of experiences and successes. They are yours to use, providing an easy starting point in your 609 dispute journey.

But our journey doesn't end here. While the templates serve as sturdy outposts, aiding you in your quest for justice and rectification, knowing how to craft your own dispute letter is akin to having a tailor-made armor that breathes life into your unique dispute.

In the quest for credit repair, one size does not fit all. The personal intricacies and unique contexts surrounding your dispute necessitate a dispute letter that is just as unique, just as personal, and just as precise. Knowing how to craft your tailored dispute letter allows you to engage with your own financial narrative more effectively, empowering you to navigate any questionable entries with improved confidence and ability.

So strap in for a thorough excavation into the eloquent art of dispute letters, as we guide you through crafting the perfect 609 dispute letter from the ground up. Your journey to credit score restoration has never been more poised for success, and we're thrilled to be with you every step of the way.

Penned with persuasive precision, these letters become a powerful tool earnestly bridging the gap between credit report errors and their rightful resolution.

The Backdrop: Setting the Stage for a 609 Dispute Letter

Whenever suspicious or unfamiliar entries become evident on your credit report, a sense of alarm might settle in. But remember, a perfectly crafted 609 dispute letter is your ally in contesting these inaccuracies, effectively opening doors to their investigation and potential rectification.

Consider Alice, an ardent gardener who recently noticed her credit score withering away like a neglected plant. Amid tightly managed expenses and diligent repayments, credit report errors had quietly intruded into her financial portrait, silently but steadily gnawing her credit score. For Alice, a well-structured and persuasive 609 Dispute Letter serves as the watering can, offering a chance to nourish her credit score back to health.

Painting a Persuasive Picture: The Essence of a 609 Letter

The power of language manifests itself through the persuasive strength of a well-crafted dispute letter. Strategic crafting of the letter, not just disputes arguments, but also calls for attention, ignites curiosity, and encourages the bureau to act. Navigating this delicate endeavor means mastering tactful persuasion and upholding absolute authenticity.

Balancing a fine line between assertion and aggression is crucial. Embody an assertive tone that underscores your seriousness, yet maintains a respectful disposition toward the credit bureaus. The careful weaving of this intricate tapestry of ethos, empathy, and accuracy captures the essence of crafting the perfect 609 dispute letter.

Precision in Detail: Displaying the Discerning Eye

Details become the lifeblood of a 609 dispute letter. Begin by ensuring that your coincidence details are accurate and up-to-date. Then, start dissecting your credit report. For each contested entry, provide an itemized explanation, clearly describing why the entry is erroneous. Remember, the more details you can provide, the more robust your case becomes.

Let's return to Alice's story, whose credit report showed an unfamiliar credit line drawn. In her dispute letter, she meticulously detailed the entry in question, explicitly describing why it was erroneous and not linked to any financial activity she had performed. Alice's precise detailing ignited the curiosity of the bureau, persuading them to launch an investigation into the contested item.

Bolstering your Case: Leveraging Supporting Evidence

Substantiating your claims with evidence takes your dispute letter a notch higher. If you have documentation that disproves the erroneous entry, include it. These proofs could range from bank statements, payment receipts to written documents, all serving as silver bullets capably disarming inaccuracies off your report.

Alice was able to find an old bank statement that clearly contradicted the suspected credit line in her report. Attaching this as evidence fortified her dispute, adding layers of credibility to her letter and substantially bolstering her case.

Closing with Conviction: The Powerful Last Impression

Ending your dispute letter on a decisive note underlines your assertion and leaves a lasting impact. Ensure you incorporate a formal request for the removal of the disputed item after rectification. You might also ask for a written confirmation after the rectification. This displays your conviction and your keen interest in timely and accurate credit reporting.

Keeping these key elements in mind, Alice crafted her 609 letter that successfully highlighted the inaccuracies in her credit report. Leveraging persuasive precision and backed by damning evidence, her dispute letter ensured an investigation was initiated that eventually led to the rectification of the erroneous entries. This journey underscores a well-crafted dispute letter's power, forming the cornerstone of effective credit repair.

Crafting a perfect 609 dispute letter is a nuanced exercise in strategy, precision, and persuasion. It incorporates the three Cs - Clear, Concise, and Convincing. Hence, it's essential to meticulously craft your dispute letter, armed with detailed explanations, strong evidence, and a clear request for rectification - your secret formula to unlocking successful credit repair.

6.3 Successful Case Studies Using 609 Letters

The power of a well-crafted 609 Dispute Letter lies not only in its theory and legalities but also in the positive outcomes it has brought to countless individuals, assuaging their financial anxieties and uplifting their credit scores. To illuminate the transformative potential of these letters, we delve now into actual cases where 609 dispute letters have been used to great success.

Reclaiming Financial Stability With a Clean Slate

Let's start with the story of Jane, a diligent working single mother from Austin, Texas. Jane, like so many others, had grappled with a failing credit score due to disputed late payments from a credit card she never owned. Despite several attempts to remove this inaccurate information, the stubborn blot sabotage her credit report.

Upon discovering 609 dispute letters, Jane downloaded and personalized our template. Brimming with newfound hope, she detailed the inaccuracies, demanded an investigation, and sought validation with a fiery determination in her letter. Weeks later, she received a response confirming the removal of the late payments from her report. Not only did her score elevate, but her ability to secure better interest rates improved. Jane's success exemplifies the potency and the impact of 609 dispute letters - a lifeline in the choppy waters of credit repair.

The Power of Persistence

Next, we have Brian, a young man from Denver whose journey with 609 dispute letters serves as a testament to the power of persistence. Brian's credit score was laden with collection fees from a medical bill mishandled by his insurance. While the first 609 dispute letter he sent resulted in a polite denial from the bureau, Brian refused to buckle under the roadblock. He realized that repetition and persistence were allies in his journey to credit restoration.

He analyzed his situation, restructured and replicated his 609 dispute letter. His persistent endeavor struck a chord with the credit bureau. They agreed to launch a thorough investigation, which, by the third attempt, led to the removal of the medical bill's collection fees from his report. Brian's FICO score was free from the chain of inaccuracies, and he was able to secure the car loan he had been diligently saving for. Brian's patience and perseverance embody the fortitude required in credit repair - it can seem laborious, but the fruits of success are sweet.

Rising from the Rubble: A Tale of Credit Redemption

A glimpse into the story of Patricia, a retiree from Seattle whose credit score had deteriorated due to an unexpected job loss, provides a nuanced perspective of 609 dispute letters. Patricia plunged into financial uncertainty, resulting in a scam related charge-off on her credit report. Overwhelmed and desperate to rebuild her financial stability, she discovered the 609 dispute letter.

After persistent attempts and employing a customized 609 dispute letter explaining her situation in detail, the bank recognized Patricia's predicament. As a result, they agreed to retract the charge-off from her report. At the dawn of retirement, Patricia was able to secure a refinance for her home loan, significantly easing her financial burden. Patricia's story illuminates hope amidst despair and stands as a beacon to anyone teetering on the edges of financial stability.

Each story illustrates that with the right tools and perseverance, obstacles that once seemed insurmountable can recede, making way for financial growth and freedom. Each case represents individuals like you; hard-working parents, young adults establishing credit, or aspiring homeowners. All were united by their drive to alleviate financial stress, regain control over their financial futures, and secure a sense of liberty and security. Thus demonstrating, the profound potential of the 609 dispute letter.

Of course, it's essential to remember that the journey to credit restoration is individual and unique – our paths may be different, but our destination of financial freedom and strength is shared.

In conclusion, 609 dispute letters are not just a pile of regulations and assertions. These real-life testimonials instill the belief: with the knowledge and the willpower, you can reshape your financial destiny.

6.4 Strategies for Response and Follow-up

Crafting and submitting a well-researched and compelling 609 dispute letter is a critical first step in securing a better credit score. However, regardless of how stellar your letter may be, it's essential to be prepared for the response process and capitalizing on follow-up actions. By embracing the strategies detailed here, you can not only increase the likelihood of your dispute's success but also climb one step closer to financial freedom.

A Patient Understanding: Timeframes and Expectations

Recognizing that credit bureaus have a finite window to review disputes is fundamental to the follow-up phase. Under the Fair Credit Reporting Act (FCRA), bureaus are legally required to investigate disputes within 30 days of receiving them. Sometimes, the response may take longer - acknowledging this timeline can minimize frustration and ensure a level-headed approach to responding.

Decoding the Response: Analyzing Credit Bureau Decisions

Upon receiving the bureau's response, take the time to carefully analyze it. There are three possible outcomes:

Success: Your request is approved, and inaccuracies are either removed or rectified.
Rejection: The bureau disagrees with your findings, and no action is taken.
Insufficient Investigation: The bureau may lack enough information to resolve the dispute fully.

For scenarios one and three, it's crucial to verify whether updates have been applied to your credit report correctly. This step ensures that the changes you worked for are accurately reflected in your credit score.

When Persistence Pays Dividends: Responding to Rejection

If your dispute is rejected, as may happen on occasion, it's crucial not to be disheartened. First, consider whether the evidence you provided was sufficient. If relevant, collect further documentation and specifics to submit a detailed follow-up dispute. Recalibrate your 609 dispute letter, addressing the bureau's concerns, and reiterating your request.

In your response, consider incorporating verified resources that fortify your dispute, including documentation from original creditors or verified legal documents. By bolstering your case and blending determination with persistence, you may elicit a more favorable outcome in the subsequent review.

Follow-up Etiquette: Making Your Voice Heard

Following up with bureaus after the initial 30-day window has passed, but without the response yet, can demonstrate your commitment to resolving the dispute. To track the case's progress, you can visit the credit bureau's online submission portals or contact customer support representatives to inquire about your case's status. Patient follow-ups keep your dispute fresh in both your mind and the bureau's, ensuring the matter isn't forgotten.

Building a Bridge: Connecting with Creditors

While your primary correspondence is with credit bureaus, engaging with creditors can facilitate a more comprehensive resolution. By cultivating meaningful relationships with creditors and understanding their perspective, you foster an environment conducive to collaboration. Tangibly, this can lead to accelerated debt repayment plans, reduced fees, or a more favorable reporting outcome.

Taking Matters to the Next Level: Escalations

In rare instances, it may become necessary to escalate your dispute beyond the typical response and follow-up cycle. If no progress can be discerned or if you suspect negligence or deceit on the bureau's part, it might be time to involve a regulatory body. The Consumer Financial Protection Bureau (CFPB) exists to protect consumers by regulating disputes related to inaccuracies in credit reports. By reaching out to the CFPB, you amplify the visibility of your case and activate a higher level of oversight.

Through diligent preparation, strategizing your response efforts, and capitalizing on efficient follow-up, you can ensure your dispute journey is fruitful, increasing the likelihood of elevating your credit score and securing financial freedom—embracing each aspect of the process signals your commitment to repair your credit health effectively.

In conclusion, appropriately responding to and pursuing follow-up actions after submitting your 609 dispute letter can be the key to finalizing your financial transformation. From understanding timelines to escalating disputes when necessary, adopting these methods ensures you make every effort to maximize your chances of rectifying errors on your credit report and achieving financial freedom.

Chapter 7:
The Art of Disputing: Navigating the Creditor-Lender Battlefield

7.1 Comprehending your Rights under FCRA

The Fair Credit Reporting Act (FCRA), enacted in 1970, serves as a foundational piece of legislation that empowers and protects consumers in the arena of credit reporting. Understanding your rights under this landmark law is pivotal for any individual embarking on a journey to repair or maintain their credit score. By comprehending both your rights and the tools available to you under the FCRA, you become better equipped to confidently navigate the intricate creditor-lender battlefield and rebuild your path to financial freedom.

Empowering the Consumer: Core Principles of the FCRA

The FCRA was designed to protect the privacy and rights of consumers in the realm of credit reporting. To provide a comprehensive framework, the law defines various rights and limitations for both consumers and credit reporting agencies. It was established on several key principles:

- **Accuracy**: Ensuring that the information included in a credit report is accurate, complete, and up-to-date.
- **Privacy**: Safeguarding the consumer's personal information from unauthorized or unlawful use.
- **Fairness**: Encouraging responsible information sharing among credit reporting agencies, creditors, and other entities.
- **Transparency**: Facilitating open communication and understanding between credit reporting agencies and consumers.

These principles serve as the bedrock of consumer rights under the FCRA. A thorough grasp of these tenets, coupled with practical knowledge of how they are applied, empowers you to assert your rights more effectively and make informed decisions related to your credit health.

Uncovering your Rights: Key FCRA Provisions

Having established the underlying values of the FCRA, it's essential to dive deeper into specific rights afforded to consumers. By exploring these provisions, you gain insight into the protections and tools available for individuals navigating the complexities of the credit reporting system.

Right to Access: Consumers have the right to request and access a free copy of their credit report once every 12 months from each of the major credit reporting agencies: Equifax, Experian, and TransUnion.

Accuracy: Credit reporting agencies are required to ensure that their records are accurate and up-to-date. Inaccurate or obsolete information, such as collection accounts, charge-offs, and bankruptcies that have exceeded their statute of limitations, must be removed.

Dispute Rights: If you believe that there is inaccurate information in your credit report, you have the right to dispute these inaccuracies. Credit reporting agencies have a legal obligation to investigate disputes within 30 days, and they must remove or correct any unsubstantiated or erroneous information.

Resolving Errors: If the investigation reveals that your dispute is valid, the credit reporting agency is required to correct the information or delete the disputed entry from your report. You also have the right to request that the agency notify all those who have received your report in the past six months of the changes made.

Notification of Adverse Action: If an adverse action (e.g., loan denial, higher interest rate) is taken against you as a result of information in your credit report, you have the right to be informed of the specific reason(s) for the adverse action. This notification includes the name, address, and phone number of the credit reporting agency responsible for providing the information.

Inclusion of a Consumer Statement: If you feel that your dispute has not been resolved to your satisfaction, you have the right to add a 100-word statement to your credit report, outlining your perspective on the disputed information. This statement will be presented to anyone who accesses your credit report in the future, ensuring that your viewpoint is considered.

Embracing FCRA: A Launchpad for Financial Growth
By comprehending your rights under the FCRA, you become better positioned to challenge inaccurate information in your credit report, hold credit reporting agencies accountable, and

protect your financial future. The process of learning about and leveraging these rights translates into a more robust arsenal of tools to help you repair or maintain your credit score. Ultimately, embracing the rights enshrined by the FCRA can be a springboard for attaining financial freedom and embarking on a path toward financial security and peace of mind.

7.2 Techniques for Successful Disputes

As you grapple with the formidable task of rebuilding your credit landscape, throwing yourself headfirst into the fray is seldom productive. Instead, it is a strategic maneuvering that helps you navigate the precarious world of credit disputes. This journey is akin to a chess game; understanding the rulebook is only the beginning. To triumph on the checkered board of financial disputes, you need to master a repertoire of tactical moves and strategic plays.

Strive for Precision

All matters related to your credit report revolve around accuracy. When you initiate a dispute, ensure your arguments are bulletproof. An impenetrable dispute is built on precision, rooting out inconsistencies and errors in your credit report. Highlight these discrepancies with irrefutable evidence. Cite specific lines, entries, or transactions in your report that contain errors and validate your statements with supporting documents. Your steadfast dedication to precision manifests as a formidable challenge for lenders and credit bureaus, compelling them to remedy unwarranted errors.

Prioritize Disputes Wisely

In a perfect world, you would be able to dispute every negative entry off your credit report expeditiously. However, in reality, credit bureaus are overwhelmed with disputes; their overburdened systems can often lead to delayed resolutions. To amplify your success in clearance, be judicious about choosing your battles and wisely prioritize your disputes. Dispute entries that weigh heavily on your credit score first. Identity theft, inaccurate account statuses, incorrect balances, and wrongly attributed late payments are areas worth focusing on first.

Procure the Right Tools

Making substantial headway through the dispute process requires more than sheer determination— you need to equip yourself with the right tools. Master the art of letter writing, an overlooked but critical aspect of credit repair. A well-crafted dispute letter is your battle cry on this battlefield. It should be clear, concise, and compelling, combining facts and persuasiveness in a delicate dance. Equally crucial is understanding the digital channels available for dispute resolution, such as the online platforms provided by credit bureaus. Your proficiency in both paper and digital dispute methods ensures that you're equipped to traverse any terrain on this battlefield.

Pursue Diligently, But Patiently

Persistence is key in this journey. A single dispute letter might not clinch victory. There will be setbacks, ignored disputes, and prolonged resolutions. But remember, just like a chess game, this is a test of resilience and strategic patience— not of swift, frantic movements. You must be persistent without falling into the trap of frustration, always keeping your eyes on the ultimate goal: a clean, healthy credit report. If your disputes are continually ignored, consider more formal escalation, such as involving the Consumer Financial Protection Bureau (CFPB) or legal representation.

Practice Empathy and Professionalism

Likewise, maintaining an attitude of professionalism, empathy, and respect towards the recipient of your disputes is paramount. Remember, your dispute letters or calls are handled by overworked employees operating within a rigid system. While their lack of responsiveness may not appear fair, fostering an angry or confrontational attitude rarely accelerates a resolution. Practice empathy; consider the challenges they face, and always uphold professionalism in your communication, increasing the likelihood of a positive outcome.

Ultimately, the practice of successful disputing is an art, not a messy, haphazard brawl. It consists of a dance between precision and patience, balance and boldness, strategy, and sensitivity. As you march forward on this journey, keep these techniques close at hand. They serve as your shield and sword in this battlefield.

Keep in mind your journey, as challenging as it may seem now, is not without its rewards. The endgame is not just a simple victory in a dispute or the removal of a negative credit entry— but rather a sweeping transformation, a metamorphosis of your financial profile from the ashes of credit despair to the fertile soils of financial freedom.

7.3 Picking your Battles: When to Dispute

As you delve into the trenches of credit disputes, a near overflow of imperfections, errors, and issues can be unearthily dug up like old, buried bones in hallowed ground. Your financial skeletons untouched for years may suddenly be flung into the stark light of scrutiny.

However, in the unfolding battlefield of credit disputes, it is pivotal to understand that not every battle is worth fighting. This is because time and resources are finite, fighting every spat over minutiae may lead to bigger, more influential credit issues being overlooked.

So how can you decode when to strap on your armor and ride into battle and when to let minor transgressions slide? This requires delicate finesse and understanding, as challenging and disputing can have its ramifications.

The Significance of an Error

First and foremost, consider the weightage of the error. An incorrect address or a misspelled name may not impact your credit score but can hint at deeper issues of identity theft. On the other hand, errors like late payments, wrongful charge-offs, or an account that doesn't belong to you can bear tremendous consequences for your credit score. Every issue is not just an error. It is a knot in the fabric of your creditworthiness, some knots undoubtedly matter more than others.

For instance, Mark, an aspiring homeowner, spotted a discrepancy in the length of his credit history on his report. A credit card account opened while he was in university showed up as recent. Although a relatively minor issue, it was slicing away precious points from his credit score. On disputing, Mark won an impressive 15-point boost to his score. This tale underscores the importance of understanding error significance and selecting your battles wisely.

Impact on Future Credit Applications

Another point to ponder while picking your battles is your immediate future financial ambitions. Are you planning to apply for a significant loan, like a mortgage, or a premium credit card in the near future? In this scenario, even minor discrepancies can result in a devastating ripple effect. A single negative tick on your credit report could be the cause for a denied loan application or higher interest rates, tarnishing your financial excellence.

Emily, a single mother, was close to realizing her dream of owning a house. Spotting a couple of inaccuracies, including a wrongly attributed late payment and an incorrectly listed credit limit, Emily decided to dispute these errors. This strategic move resulted in a more favorable mortgage deal. Emily's story embroiders the importance of considering your future credit aspirations while picking your battles.

The Cost-Benefit of Disputing

The world of credit disputes is not a sprint but rather an endurance race. It's essential to weigh the cost-benefit ratio before diving into a dispute. How much time, energy, and possibly money are you willing to invest in a dispute, and what could be the estimated return on your investment? If the return is a worthwhile improvement in your credit score or savings on interest rates, then charge headfirst into the maelty fray. If the benefit is marginal and you are battling an already strained schedule, it might be smarter to conserve your powers for a more significant fight.

Take the case of Frank, a young professional, who spotted a tiny collection account on his report for an unpaid library fine during his college years. Although visually a tiny blip on his otherwise squeaky credit radar, this collection account was causing his score to dip. Deciding to dispute the account was a smart move as Frank added a few critical points to his score, paving the way for a better job offer awaiting credit checks. Frank's story underlines the necessity of evaluating the cost-benefit ratio while picking your disputes.

Vividly understanding the credit Norse saga, you need to define the dragons worth slaying. The journey is marked with careful selection, strategic choices, and understanding the echoes of each credit discrepancy. The process of picking your battles in your credit war is as much an art as the dispute itself. Identify the red flags, evaluate their significance, foresee their impact, calculate costs and benefits, and only then, decide whether to fight or to let go.

7.4 Alternative Dispute Resolution Methods

In our financial Odyssey, sometimes we find ourselves standing at a crossroads. One road leads to a conventional dispute process - a path laid by paperwork, phone calls, and formal complaints. However, another less traveled by but just as effective route weaves through the landscape of alternative dispute resolution (ADR). In the credit realm, this intriguing alternative can be as valid and potent as any formal grievance.

Steering Away from Conventional Tactics

Alternative dispute resolution methods present a means of resolving disputes outside of the traditional red tape. These practices encompass negotiation, mediation, and arbitration and offer quick, less daunting, and often cheaper routes to dispute rectification, straying away from litigation's labyrinth.

ADR methods can drastically transform the creditor-lender battlefield, opening up new avenues for achieving your credit score "El Dorado."

The Power of Negotiation

Imagine you're Alice, who erroneously ignored credit card bills while transitioning jobs. They slipped into collections, heavily impacting her credit score. Conventional disputing might seem daunting, but Alice chose to handle this setback through negotiation. She contacted the collections agency, explaining her situation and proposing a payment plan to clear her debts. The agency, appreciating her proactive approach, agreed to report her account as 'Paid in Full.' Alice's credit report was enhanced, and she achieved a result without entering the formal dispute fray.

Negotiation is a dialogic process where conflicting parties discuss their issues to reach a mutually beneficial agreement. It's a power every credit holder wields, often underestimated and underutilized. The key lies in clear, straightforward conversation articulating your dispute, offering solutions, and demonstrating a genuine intent to resolve the issue.

Mediation: A Neutral Set of Eyes

Now envision Max, a conscientious credit card holder who found an erroneous late payment entry in his credit report. Puzzled and frustrated, he disputed the entry with his credit card company. Against expectations, the company maintained his late payment was valid.

Max decided to use mediation. He employed a neutral third party (a mediator) who facilitated a discussion between him and the company. With the mediator's help, they discovered his payment had not been processed due to a system error on part of the creditor. The company acknowledged the mistake and removed the late payment entry. Thus, mediation, a structured, interactive negotiation process, helped Max solve his dispute favorably.

Arbitration: When you Need an Adjudicator

We'll take Joshua's case: an entrepreneur with a business loan dispute. His lender mistakenly reported his loan default when he had merely asked for a repayment extension, impacting his credit score. When conventional disputing and negotiation didn't resolve the issue, he opted for arbitration.

An independent arbitrator reviewed Joshua's case, hearing both parties out. Assessing the evidence, the arbitrator deemed Joshua's report needed correcting. The lender, bound by the arbitrator's decision, rectified the reporting error. Joshua's credit score recovered, validating arbitration's potency.

Arbitration is a decision-making dispute resolution method, where a neutral party (the arbitrator) determines the fair settlement based on evidence and merit.

ADR methods can diffuse the disputes' tension, ensuring effective resolution while preserving the relationship between the creditor and the borrower. However, their success largely depends on the specific examination of the dispute, willingness of conflicting parties to participate, and the capability of the negotiator, mediator, or arbitrator.

These methods are hence effective tools for those who are not afraid to take the path less trodden. Their adoption requires courage, expertise, and empathy, all crucial nuances of the art of disputing.

As we move towards an era of financial enlightenment, ADR options encourage dialogue and co-operation over conflict. The battleground transforms into a negotiation table, the disputes into discussions, and resolutions into collaborative efforts. This evolving battlefield reflects a significant shift from adversarial to co-operative, indicating that the future of finance may not necessarily be litigious, but one embracing the human touch in a field of numbers.

Chapter 8:
Outwitting the Credit Bureaus: Insider Knowledge for an Impeccable Score

8.1 Understanding Credit Bureaus' Operation

Credit, much like a shadow, silently accompanies us throughout our financial odyssey - a ceaseless presence often unnoticed, yet greatly influencing our journey's progression. Serving as this invisible shadow's puppeteers, credit bureaus hold an unparalleled influence over our financial lives. To take control of our financial destiny, we first need to understand these puppeteers, lifting the mystifying veil that shrouds credit bureaus' operations.

Credit Bureaus: The Unseen Financial Giants

In an effort to comprehend the operational nuances of credit bureaus, we need to dive deeper into the world of credit reporting. Our story begins with the three credit titans in the United States: Experian, TransUnion and Equifax. These giants hold the reins of the consumer credit system, incessantly monitoring and evaluating us.

You might wonder why these institutions wield so much control. To put it succinctly, lenders and creditors rely heavily on credit bureaus to assess borrowers' creditworthiness before any financial negotiations. They are the eyes that scrutinize your financial persona, dictating your lending potential and your credit capabilities.

Gathering the 'Credit Intel': A Watchful Eye

Your credit journey starts when you participate in credit transactions, a noteworthy corner in your financial escapades. Be it availing a loan, a credit card, or making a substantial payment commitment, each economic action you take is an exhibit under credit bureaus' studious gaze.

These agencies, by virtue of the Fair Credit Reporting Act (FCRA), are legally authorized to mine your financial data. They assemble a comprehensive credit report by pooling information from lenders, collection agencies, government agencies, and public records. This report, a digital ledger of your financial history, includes your borrowing habits, repayment consistency, existing debts, personal information, and any legal actions tied to your financial behavior.

From Data to Ratings: The Credit Score Alchemy

Pivoting from mere spectators to influential adjudicators, credit bureaus employ complex algorithms to translate your data into a numeric expression: your credit score. This process of credit score alchemy is unique to each bureau, but they use similar elements: the FICO score components. Consisting of your payment history, credit utilization, credit history length, credit mix, and new credit, the concoction of these factors ends up becoming your magic number.

Bureaus then substantiate your financial potential into a three-digit score ranging from 300 to 850. The closer you are to 850, the more lucrative financial possibilities unfold for you, reinforcing the importance and influence of these credit scores.

The Conduit between Borrowers and Lenders: Information Highways

Experian, TransUnion, and Equifax function as vital information highways in a vast, intricate network encompassing various financial service providers. Lenders, insurers, employers, and landlords often turn to these bureaus to access an individual's credit data and make informed decisions based on that information.

For example, a mortgage lender peruses the potential borrower's credit report and score to analyze their ability to honor the loan obligations. An employer might evaluate an applicant's trustworthiness by analyzing their credit behavior. The bureaus connect and influence these critical decision-making processes, thereby reinforcing their role as information hubs in our financial wheel.

The Cycle of Reporting: A Cyclical Score Symphony

Your financial journey doesn't exist in a vacuum. It's part of a dynamic, cyclical score symphony orchestrated by credit bureaus. As you go about your financial course, your transactions and behaviors stir reactions in the credit universe. These reactions are then caught, documented and evaluated by credit bureaus. The resulting scores and reports initiate further financial decisions, both by you and the involved financial institutions. This incessant evaluation and impact cycle is the essence of the credit bureaus' operation.

Understanding how credit bureaus operate transforms a seeming quagmire into a navigable roadmap for effective credit enhancement. Knowing what information they document, how your transactions influence your credit report, the significance of your credit score, and the role of these bureaus in decision making, equips you with the intelligence to outmaneuver pitfalls and strategize your financial maneuvers. The goal isn't to defeat the credit bureaus; instead, it's to coexist, making these giants your allies, not adversaries.

8.2 Their Weaknesses, Your Gains

Amid the financial interplay, credit bureaus are often perceived as invincible gatekeepers, holding the keys to a wellspring of financial opportunities. Their power appears dominant, compensating for their elusive operation by reflecting their influence in every credit score. However, it is essential to remember that these financial behemoths are not impervious, and acknowledging the chinks in their armor can enable you to transform their weaknesses into your financial gains.

The Flaw in the Machinery: Credit Reporting Errors

The first notable weakness in the credit bureau's systematic operation is related to credit reporting errors. Despite their meticulous gathering of a vast data spectrum, inaccuracies can seep into your credit reports through numerous negligence conduits. A study by the Federal Trade Commission disclosed that one in four consumers found errors on their credit reports that might have impacted their credit scores.

You might wonder, how do these inaccuracies creep into your meticulous financial document? The errors can sprout from various sources: an incompatible piece of information from a financial institution, a misinterpretation of a digit during data entry, confusing your data with someone bearing a similar name, or as blatant as identity theft, leading to erroneous entries.

For the financial aspirant striving to improve their credit score, these inaccuracies pose a substantial opportunity. It offers the chance to identify, dispute, and rectify these errors, paving the path for an improved credit score. The burden of credit reporting errors, thus, transforms into an advantage for the resourceful credit seeker.

The Cycle of Data: Time as Your Ally

The second notable chink in the credit bureau's facade is time. The lifecycle of debt is an immutable reality in credit operations. Negative information like late payments, defaults, and collection activities won't haunt your credit history indefinitely. Most derogatory information shows an expiration date of seven years from the initial delinquency date, with the exception of bankruptcy, which can linger for up to a decade.

⧗ Debt Time Limits

Debt Type	Time Limit	Impact on Credit Report	Impact on Credit Score
Credit Card Debt	3-6 years (depending on state)	Up to 7 years from date of last activity	Medium - Can significantly lower score if currently delinquent or in collections
Medical Debt	3-6 years (depending on state)	Up to 7 years from date of first delinquency	Low - Has less impact than other debt types
Federal Student Loans	20-25 years or until paid off	Remains until paid off	Medium - Late or missed payments can hurt credit scores
Auto Loans	3-6 years after repossession	Up to 7 years from date of last payment	High - Repossession severely damages credit score
Mortgages	By state, often 10-15 years	Up to 7 years from date of last payment	High - Foreclosure significantly hurts credit scores

As time progresses and you continue to engender positive credit habits, these negative elements recede into the shadows, their weight shrinks, and the fresher, healthier credit actions take the spotlight. Here, patience is not simply a virtue but a strategic tool in gradually phasing out the negative marks.

The Unexplored Territory: Limitations on Data Procured

While credit bureaus possess an extensive overview of your credit history, it's crucial to remember that they are not omnipotent. Certain aspects of your financial behavior remain undetected by these agencies. For instance, your income, your savings, the payment of utilities, savings behavior, and rental payment histories usually stay under the radar of these bureaus.

Herein lies a tactical advantage for an astute borrower. By effectively showcasing these overlooked, positive aspects of your financial attitude to lenders, you can improve your creditriety potential, regardless of the credit bureaus' assertions. Smart financial and credit managements are thus not merely confined to bending to the credit bureaus' edicts; rather, they include broadening your financial visibility to encompass positive actions that contribute to your creditworthiness.

Reforming The Underperformance: Nudging Towards Change

The momentous power of credit bureaus has not escaped regulatory influence. As recently as 2015, major credit bureaus agreed to a settlement —largely prompted by the New York Attorney General— leading to reforms in practices like error resolutions and the reporting of medical debt. Moreover, active consumer advocacy groups ceaselessly labor to bring transparency and fairness to the credit scoring system.

As an informed credit seeker, you can capitalize on this growing wave of credit bureau accountability to foster an equitable financial landscape. By staying abreast of these evolving regulations, engaging with consumer advocacy initiatives, and using legal recourse in situations of inaccuracies or unfair reporting, you can turn the tide, transforming these developments to bolster your journey to a high credit score.

In conclusion, credit bureaus, while powerful, are not infallible. Their operational constructs contain exploitable cracks, whether it's inaccuracies in credit reports, the weighting effect of time, or the limitations on data they gather. A strategic credit seeker recognizes these weak points and effectively uses them to improve their credit journey. By actively disputing errors, harnessing the power of patience, showcasing invisible creditworthy behaviors, or leveraging evolving regulatory changes, you convert their weaknesses into your gains in the pursuit of a commendable credit score.

8.3 Insider Secrets: Making Bureaus Work for You

In your journey to a stellar credit score, understanding the architecture of credit bureaus and unmasking their limitations is crucial. Yet, to truly outwit these credit guardians, you must delve deeper, master the art of making these very bureaus work favorably for you. This section reveals some insider secrets to help you transform credit bureaus from seemingly insurmountable monoliths into well-tailored allies fueling your financial prosperity.

Unlocking the Power of Multiple Bureaus

The first secret revolves around the inherent structure of the credit industry itself. While you might be familiar with the three major credit bureaus, Equifax, Experian, and TransUnion, seldom do we recognize the individuality they represent. Rather than clones, producing identical credit reports, these bureaus generate unique records due to their sources of data and recording methodology.

This realization unveils a potent strategy: diversity of credit applications. When a lender or service provider consults a bureau to check your credit score, often, they only reach out to one. Should you face disapproval from a lender due to a lower score in one credit bureau, consider reapplying with a lender known to pull from a different bureau where your score might be higher. While it involves some research to identify lenders' preferred bureaus, the results can significantly benefit your loan approval odds.

How does this approach make bureaus work for you? Every approval of credit is recorded in your credit history, contributing positively to your overall credit score. Thus, by tactically applying for credit, you're leveraging the differences between bureaus' interpretations of your creditworthiness to boost your financial prosperity.

Utilizing Bureau-Specific Dispute Platforms

Each credit bureau operates an individual dispute platform. Thus, when you detect an error in your credit report, it should be addressed with the specific bureau that lists the mistake. Yet, this insider secret goes beyond simply identifying the right dispute channels.

The potency of this secret lies in fully embracing the specificities and idiosyncrasies of the dispute platform. Each bureau's dispute mechanism varies slightly in terms of its user interface, response time, and ease of communication. Instead of approaching them with a one-size-fits-all mindset, fine-tuning your dispute approach to align with the specific bureau's system can hasten error correction.

Embracing a tailored approach might mean crafting a dispute letter that adheres to a particular bureau's format or diligently following up within the response time frames they typically operate. By embracing the intricacies of the bureau's dispute platform, you are aligning their error resolution system with your score improvement goal, ensuring quicker rectification of inaccuracies and credit score enhancement.

Leverage the Growing Role of Non-Traditional Data

Credit bureaus, recognizing their limitations on only gathering traditional financial data, are tentatively stepping into the realm of non-traditional data. The inclusion of rental repayment history, utility payments, or on-time cell phone bill payments can offer a more rounded view of one's financial responsibility, benefiting individuals with smaller credit history or those rehabilitating their creditworthiness.

Here's how you can exploit this evolving scenario. On-time utility and rental payments, though overlooked in the general credit calculation, can now become strategic inputs to bolster your credit score. You can subscribe to services that report these payments to bureaus, thereby populating your credit report with positive payment behavior. It's like telegraphing creditworthiness through channels usually invisible to the credit industries, further enhancing your overall credit profile.

Influence via Innovation: Stand Atop The Credit-Tech Wave

Technology is revolutionizing the credit industry, and those adaptive to change reap the rewards. New, innovative services grant consumers agency, letting them directly influence their credit scores. For instance, Experian Boost and UltraFICO allow users to influence their score by incorporating non-traditional data like checking account behavior or on-time utility payments.

By staying ahead of the curve and making use of these tech-enabled services, you tap into the evolving nature of credit scoring. This active approcah helps you shift from being a passive observer to an active participant in shaping your credit score narrative—another way to make the bureaus work for you.

In conclusion, the secret to outwitting credit bureaus lies in understanding their unique structures and workings. By taking advantage of individual bureau attributes, customizing your dispute approaches, utilizing non-traditional data, and harnessing the power of evolving credit technologies, you ensure that these agencies do more than just quantify your financial behavior; they become accomplices in your pursuit of financial prosperity.

8.4 Legal Loopholes to Better Credit: Turning the System to Your Advantage

Often, in the journey of credit improvement, we find ourselves facing monstrous walls that seem insurmountable. Wall after wall, be it inaccurate negative information, stubborn lenders, or credit bureau errors, the process can quickly feel overwhelming. But what if, rather than collisions, these walls could be gateways? In this last section, we will uncover the legally sound, yet often overlooked, loopholes that can help you gain the upper hand, contributing to a superior credit scores.

Enforcing Statute of Limitations: Not Forever Bound

One of the potent legal tools within the credit system is the concept of the "statute of limitations." In layman's terms, it is the timeframe within which a lender or collector can sue for an unpaid debt. The value of this concept lies in the understanding that not all debts bind you forever. In fact, the statute of limitations varies by state and the type of debt, often ranging from three to six years.

Imagine this: perhaps a forgotten credit card debt from six years ago is still haunting your credit report, and the collector threatens to sue if you don't pay. In most states, they would be exceeding the statute of limitations, meaning they no longer have the legal right to sue for that debt. You've now discovered a loophole. By knowing your legal rights, you don't get trapped into paying an age-old debt or worse, restarting the clock on that debt by accidentally acknowledging its existence. Instead, with the statute of limitations as your shield, you can legally and ethically evade these outdated financial obligations.

Goodwill Interventions: Kindness that Scores

In life, and in the credit world, kindness often delivers surprisingly positive results. This brings us to a lesser-used loophole known as a "Goodwill Letter." A goodwill letter is essentially a request to a lender to remove a late payment mark on your credit report as an act of goodwill. Genuine and humble, these letters make a human appeal to the lender, explaining why you missed the payment, providing context to your financial hardship, and emphasizing your usual good payment behavior.

Given that late payments can significantly lower credit scores, leveraging this loophole can potentially lead to a score increase, especially if the lender considers your request and removes the blemish. Yet, the goodwill intervention is not just about appealing to a lender's kindness. It's about revealing the responsible borrower beneath a single mistake—transforming your struggles into a narrative that fosters understanding and negotiation, ultimately creating an avenue for credit score enhancement.

Credit Bureaus' Responsibility: Validation is Key

Credit bureaus serve as the guardians and narrators of your credit history, yet they are not infallible. According to the Fair Credit Reporting Act (FCRA), you have the legal right to dispute inaccuracies in your credit report. The catch here is that these reports must be validated by the bureaus with original creditors within 30 days.

What happens if it's not validated within that period? Well, then we stumble upon another legal loophole. If the credit bureau fails to validate the debt within 30 days, by law, they are required to remove the disputed entry from your credit report. This tactic is not about exploiting the system; instead, it makes the system uphold its responsibility towards timely and accurate credit reporting, indirectly purging your report of inaccurate negativity.

The Hush that Scores: Pay-for-Delete Agreements

The last loophole in our arsenal is a strategy known as a "Pay-For-Delete" agreement. In theory, it's a fairly straightforward concept: you agree to pay the debt, if and only if, the lender or collector, in return, agrees to remove the negative entry from your credit report. Given the weightage of negative entries (late payments, charge-offs, collections) on your credit score, a successful pay-for-delete agreement can significantly enhance your score.

Though credit bureaus frown upon such practices, viewing them as a misrepresentation of one's credit history, it's not illegal. It's simply a negotiation between two parties that can lead to credit improvement. Through strategic negotiation, patience, and being aware of both your rights and limitations, you can leverage this loophole to work in your favor.

In conclusion, every credit journey involves tackling bumps and roadblocks with tenacity and resilience. Yet, sprinkling some insider knowledge and exploiting legal loopholes within the credit system can provide you with a significant advantage. From enforcing the statute of limitations and crafting goodwill letters to holding credit bureaus accountable for validation, and negotiating pay-for-delete agreements, these legal pathways can fortify your credit repair strategy – making the journey less daunting and more invigorating.

Chapter 9:
Negotiation Mastery: Shrewd Techniques to Settle Debts & Wipe Out Liens

---

9.1 Essential Negotiation Techniques

There's a specter that hangs over each person burdened by debt. It's a tormenting ghost that thrives on anxiety and panic while stifering hope of financial stability. Terms like "debt settlement" become boons rather than bane for individuals burdened by accumulating debts and plummeting credit scores.

However, settling a debt is not as straightforward as making a payment. It involves a complex, often intimidating dance — a process popularly known as negotiation. This can feel overwhelming or even hopeless, especially to those struggling financially and emotionally. We are here to change those emotions into empowerment, transforming the anxiety-ridden battle field into a manageable chess game, demonstrating the Essential Negotiation Techniques to relieve the burden of debt.

The Art of Preparation: How Understanding Your Debt Makes a Difference

Proper negotiation, strangely enough, begins before the conversation even starts. It starts with a deep comprehension of your debt, the nature of what you owe, and who you owe it to. It's about understanding who your creditor is, be it an original lender or a collection agency that has purchased your debt. Grasping the ins and outs of your debt sets you on a footing that is not only firm, but also helps you anticipate your creditor's possible moves.

Assign some quality time for this debt analysis. Go through the fine print of your debt agreement, review your credit reports, verify the legitimacy of the collections, unearth potential inaccuracies, and validate the current status of your debt (time-barred or not). Your understanding of your debt landscape forms the cornerstone of your negotiation strategy.

Framing the Narrative: Storytelling as a Negotiation Tool

Once your preparation has laid the foundation, you embark on the next step - engaging your creditor or the collections agency. The conversation that ensues is a narrative — your narrative. Your credit score, good or bad, is a story that the numbers tell. Your role, however, is to provide color - to shape that narrative to give these numbers context and to plea for understanding and lenience.

Debt Settlement Negotiation Process

1 Analyze Debt
Understand who the creditor is, debt details, validity

2 Prepare Argument
Gather evidence, draft repayment plan, know your rights

3 Initial Contact
Phone or letter requesting to negotiate debt

4 Negotiation
Discuss situation, make reasonable settlement offers

5 Agreement Finalized
Have detailed terms in writing

6 Make Payment
Pay as per agreement

Follow-up post payment to ensure credit report reflects settlement

Strike a tone that's neither too desperate nor nonchalant. Maintain an air of respectful resolution. If you've missed payments because of financial hardship, medical problems or job loss, discuss it earnestly. Personalize your negotiation. Let them know that the delinquency was not willful neglect but a consequence of uncontrollable circumstances. Often, creditors respond positively when they sense your genuine commitment towards a resolution.

Mind Games: Emotional Intelligence and Mental Fortitude

Negotiations are mind games. Understanding your emotional responses, keeping them in check, and interpreting your opponent's emotional state are critical skills to master when negotiating debt settlements. Your mental fortitude allows you to be resilient under pressure and persistent even if initial attempts don't succeed.

Always remember, collections agents are people too, trained to get under your skin. They might use tactics like humiliation or fear to stir up emotions and pressurize you into making impulsive decisions. Stay mindful of your emotional state, and assertively express your intent to settle the debt within your means.

Seeing Through the Bluff: Recognizing Creditor's Tactics

Your creditors have their tactics, and understanding them arms you with the knowledge to counter-act strategically. They might attempt to pressure you by stating that immediate full payment is the only solution, dismiss your offer outright, or threaten legal action. These are pressure tactics designed to disorient and dominate.

Being aware of these tactics, you can counter them with calmness and patience, to avoid succumbing to their intimidating strategies. Remember that, quite often, compromise is a more reasonable and preferred option for your creditors as well, considering the hassle and cost of legal proceedings. Remind them of this subtly.

Compromise is King: The Give-and-Take Formula

Negotiation is the art of compromise, the game where give-and-take is key. Here, you propose a reasonable settlement amount, maybe 50% of what you owe, and brace for counteroffers. It's a process that requires patience, understanding, and strategic flexibility. Be prepared to incrementally increase your offer but do have a line drawn in your mind that you cannot cross financially.

It's essential to remember, debt settlement might provide immediate relief but could still impact your credit score negatively. However, it provides you a footing to start rebuilding your financial health, not to mention the sigh of relief from finally being free of a lingering, suffocating debt.

In conclusion, settling debts involves strategic planning and careful negotiation. It entails arming oneself with the right knowledge about the debt, utilizing storytelling as a negotiation technique, honing emotional intelligence, understanding the creditors' tactics and mastering the art of compromise. These essential negotiation techniques are not just tools to be used in this one scenario; consider them as skills added to your life-long arsenal, a repertoire that would serve you in other facets of life where negotiation is fundamental.

9.2 Dealing with Aggressive Collectors

It's a familiar drill: the phone rings, you glance at the caller ID, and your heart sinks. It's the relentless debt collector who is making your life increasingly uncomfortable. If you're grappling with overdue debts and clawing back your financial equilibrium, dealing with aggressive collectors may feel uphill, taxing, and often emotionally draining.

If you find yourself in such a predicament, it's crucial to find an effective approach to dealing with intimidating collectors. Understanding the rules of the game, invoking your rights, and deploying shrewd negotiation tactics can enable you to restore peace in your life.

The Ground Rules: Understanding the Fair Debt Collection Practices Act

In the grand theater of debt negotiation and collection, there exists a set of ground rules enshrined in the Fair Debt Collection Practices Act (FDCPA). This legislation delineates what behavior is permissible for debt collectors and which aren't. Simply put, knowing the rules can provide a protective shield against overzealous agents.

Debt collectors' actions are controlled under the FDCPA. They are not allowed to harass you, make false statements, or engage in unfair practices. For instance, calling at unreasonable hours, threatening with arrest, or trying to collect more than you owe are clear violations of the FDCPA. Playing this card strategically can often result in collectors reassessing their approach and dealing with you respectfully.

Calling their Bluff: Turning the Tables

Standing tall when confronted by an aggressive collector is not an act of audacity, but of self-defense and dignity. It's about calling their bluff, setting boundaries and refusing to be trampled on. You have every right to question a collector's claims, to demand proof of the debt, and to discuss a repayment plan that works for you.

Verifying the debt, for instance, is an intelligent first step. You have a right to request a written validation notice, which includes the amount you owe, the name of the creditor, and instructions for challenging the debt. Ensuring the amount and authority of the debt can put the ball back in your court, prompting the collector to be reevaluative, and possibly more accommodating.

Channeling Your Inner Diplomat: The Art of Fair Negotiation

Remember, each interaction with your debt collector should represent a step toward a solution, not merely a shuffle in the deadlock. Adopt a fair negotiation approach, which is, in essence, a delicate balance between pure restraint and assertiveness. Your goal is to work towards a mutually agreeable solution, armed with all your knowledge, without losing your composure.

An aggressive collector might be intimidating, but they're just messengers for the original creditor. Behind their tough exterior, they also understand that securing a reasonable payment from you is much more productive than hounding for a full payment that you're unable to make. Be honest about your financial situation, back it with evidence, and propose a workable repayment plan.

Time's Up: Drawing the Line

Sometimes, it might be necessary to restrict a debt collector's access to you. You may limit the timing or method of these communications, or in dire circumstances, cease them altogether. Under the FDCPA, you can instruct a collection agency to communicate only through letters, which offers you the chance to gather your thoughts, consult a professional if needed, and respond maturely and strategically.

If you opt for a cease communication letter, understand the implications. While it may prevent collectors from contacting you, it does not eliminate the debt. It might expedite the collector's decision to sue you to collect the debt. Use this option wisely and only after careful consideration or legal consultation.

In sum, dealing with aggressive collectors calls for a measured blend of strategic acumen, emotional control, and legal awareness. Understanding your rights under the FDCPA, debunking the debt collector's intimidating tactics, practicing sensible negotiation, and setting firm restrictions can help you manage these interactions more confidently and effectively.

To tackle this issue meticulously, you may refer to resources such as the Consumer Financial Protection Bureau or seek professional help from debt counselors or attorneys. They can provide personalized assistance to deal with your unique circumstances.

9.3 Outsmart and Eliminate Liens

Facing a lien, especially if it's the first time, can be both challenging and intimidating. Financial setbacks can sometimes lead to situations where creditors legally claim our assets to serve as a guarantee for unpaid debts. However, it is crucial to remember that you are not without options or defenses. With a calculated combination of smart strategies, patience, and understanding, you can outflank liens and substantially reduce, negotiate, or even eliminate them altogether.

Lien: Breaking Down the Jargon

Before trying to outsmart liens, let's peel back and understand their essence. A lien, in simple terms, is a legal claim or a "hold" on some type of property—real estate, personal property, vehicles, or other assets— as a recourse for a debt. It provides creditors a pathway to seize your assets in the event you default on an obligation.

Understanding this definition is the first shield of your armor because when we clearly understand what we are up against, half the battle is won.

Make Informed Decisions - Know the Lien Type

The type of lien placed against your assets makes a considerable difference in how you approach it. There are various types of liens, including voluntary or involuntary and statutory or consensual. Voluntary liens, such as mortgage loans, are those that you willingly accept. When it comes to involuntary liens, you have tax liens, mechanic's liens, and judgment liens, which are set by creditors without your consent.

Knowing your lien type will guide your course of action. For instance, with a tax lien, you deal directly with the respective taxing entity, whereas, with judgment liens, a deep dive into the paperwork might provide insights about potential errors that can be strong points of dispute.

Damage Control - Prevent Further Liens

While it may seem knee-jerk to directly jump to the eliminating-liens phase, consider this an important caveat – try to intercept and prevent further liens. This is critical damage control that may necessitate reforming your financial habits, tightening your expenditure, and structuring a strict budget. Unrestrained spendings may snowball into larger debts and potential additional liens.

Taking Action - Removing Liens

Strategically jabbing at the liens will bear fruits only with a thorough, methodical approach. The path you decide to tread will vary depending upon the lien, the creditor, and your financial situation.

For instance, if you're dealing with a tax lien, reaching out to the government department in question to discuss your debts is beneficial. Opting for a repayment plan or an Offer in Compromise (OIC) can result in a release of lien. The latter provides an opportunity to settle your tax debt for less than the full amount, especially if your payment, even with a structured plan, would cause financial hardship.

Judgment liens, typically resultant of lawsuits, demand a keen eye for detail. Law is human-designed and hence can be marred with errors. Any error, no matter how minute, can turn the case in your favor. Review your lawsuit paperwork, identify discrepancies, such as wrong property description or incorrect lien amount, and dispute them in court. This requires immaculate documentation and a thorough understanding of your local lien laws - not easy, but not impossible either.

In negotiating with other creditors, be truthful about your situation. Lenders are often more interested in the recovery of outstanding debts than property seizure. Discuss payment plans or reduced lump-sum payment options—termed as 'Debt Settlement.'

Seek Professional Assistance

Finally, while mastering lien elimination by yourself brings a sense of accomplishment, remember that professional help is always at your disposal. Financial advisors, attorneys, or a credit counseling agency can be invaluable resources. They understand the legal jargon, the court procedures, and have refined negotiation skills to navigate the labyrinth of liens and debt.

Taking on liens might seem like a David vs. Goliath saga, but remember, David did win. Outsmarting and eliminating liens is not a pipe dream but a feasible goal with researched tactics, understanding the legal terminology, and maintaining financial discipline. It's about patiently mapping your journey, step by careful step, towards the eureka moment of eliminating liens.

9.4 Negotiating for Score Enhancement

A Game of Chess: The Art of Negotiation in Credit Improvement

A crucial factor impacting your credit score, which often remains unexplored or is not sufficiently leveraged, is the potent tool of negotiation. Negotiating with creditors isn't a widely advocated method for credit score enhancement; however, it can yield significant benefits when employed strategically. It is not about playing a winner-takes-all game with the creditors, but establishing a mutually beneficial agreement that assists in credit amelioration.

Engaging in negotiations with your creditors is akin to playing a well-thought-out game of chess. Each move, when meticulously planned, can dramatically transform your credit tableau.

The Opening Game: Understanding Your Financial Position

As in a chess game, the opening is critical when it comes to the negotiation process. Self-assessment of your financial situation forms the basis of your strategy. Assessing doesn't just mean knowing your liabilities; it encompasses understanding your repayment capacity, the time duration, and the bi-focal consideration of maintaining financial stability and enhancing the credit score simultaneously.

In tandem with your situation, understand the nature of your debts. Not all debts are the same; they may vary from revolving credit, like credit cards, to installment loans, like mortgages or auto loans, each impacting your credit score differently. An astute understanding of these aspects provides a fulcrum to your negotiation strategy.

In this opening phase, also remember the cardinal rule – never negotiate out of desperation but from a position of understanding and resolution.

The Middle Game: Navigating the Negotiation Labyrinth

The middle game forms the crux of the negotiation process. The heart of this strategy is communication. Initiate dialogue with your creditors — whether it's presenting a plausible plan for repayment, haggling over high interest rates, or discussing the possibility of reducing the overall owed amount, akin to a 'debt settlement'.

A great way to kickstart the conversation is by proposing a 'goodwill adjustment'. If you've been a good customer in the past, explaining your current financial hardships alongside presenting a precise plan of how you intend to repay might motivate creditors to remove any late payment entries from your credit report. A simple letter outlining your circumstances and showcasing your commitment to righting your financial ship can go a long way.

Simultaneously, delve into the possibility of 'pay for delete' negotiations, especially for any delinquent accounts you may have. This is a negotiation tactic where you offer to pay off the debt in full (or, in part) in exchange for the creditor consenting to remove the negative information from your credit report. Remember, this is not a strategy for evading legitimate debts but to reflect your proactive measures in taking control of your financial future.

The Endgame: Cementing the Gains

In the chess or negotiation endgame, persistence is the key. Your negotiation attempts might not succeed in the first volley. Don't let this deter you. Keep the channels of communication open and revisit your negotiation strategy if needed.

If you successfully negotiate terms with your creditors, ensure everything is documented. Agreements made over the phone might equate to word-of-mouth unless documented. Prioritize written agreements or modifications to help safeguard your interests.

Finally, commit to your negotiated plan. Renegotiated terms mean nothing if you stumble on the promised path. From the creditors' standpoint, the principal idea behind agreeing to modified terms with you is their trust in your commitment to resolving the debt.

Negotiation isn't merely about reaching an agreement; it walks hand-in-hand with rebuilding trust — the trust of creditors in your financial commitment, and more importantly, your trust in your financial resilience. Navigating this path strategically and patiently can not only help settle debts but, more importantly, repair and enhance your credit score, turning the tide in your favor.

As with any financial guide or strategy, the negotiation process emphasizes preparedness, informed strategy, and commitment. The beautiful part of playing this chess game is that over time, you become more attuned to your financial latitude and the unique dynamics of your financial ecosystem. You slowly regain control of your finances, allow your credit score to heal, and move forward toward your plan of achieving a sense of financial freedom and stability.

Chapter 10:
Fortify Your Credit Castle: Protecting Your Score from Fraud & Theft

10.1 Recognizing Credit Fraud: The First Line of Defense

Protecting your credit score from fraud and theft is akin to fortifying your castle against a potential siege. As you work hard to build and improve your creditworthiness, it's essential to stay alert and learn how to recognize credit fraud. A proactive approach is vital in safeguarding your credit reputation and ensuring long-term financial security.

⚠ Warning Signs of Credit Fraud

Type	Potential Signs	Actions to Take	Preventative Measures
Identity Theft	Unfamiliar accounts or charges, missing bills/statements	Report to financial institutions, place fraud alert	Monitor credit reports, strong passwords
Phishing Scams	Unsolicited requests for information	Do not click links or provide information	Verify legitimacy of contact
Credit Card Fraud	Unauthorized transactions, inaccurate account balances	Notify card issuer immediately	Review statements regularly
Account Takeover	Changes to account login credentials, profile, or settings	Contact financial institution to secure account	Use multifactor authentication

The Warning Signs of Credit Fraud

The ability to recognize potential fraud is vital in protecting your credit from malicious activities. Monitoring your credit reports, accounts, and card activities regularly can help you detect irregularities early on. Here are some warning signs of credit fraud that you should be aware of:

Unauthorized charges on your account statements

Keep a close eye on your credit card and bank statements and promptly report any unrecognized charges or transactions. Unauthorized charges may be a sign of fraudulent activities or, at least, incorrect billings that need to be fixed.

Unfamiliar accounts on your credit report

Regularly review your credit reports and keep an eye out for unfamiliar accounts or credit inquiries. If you spot credit cards or loans you didn't apply for, it's a red flag for potential identity theft.

Unusual communication from financial institutions or the IRS

Fraudsters often attempt to gather personal or financial information through phishing scams. Be wary of unsolicited emails, phone calls or text messages claiming to be from your bank, credit card issuer, or the IRS. These communications might request sensitive information or contain malware-laden attachments or links.

Sudden drops in your credit score without a reasonable explanation

If monitoring your credit score reveals an unexpected decrease with no reasonable explanation, conduct a thorough credit report review. It's possible that credit fraud might have negatively impacted your score.

Bills or statements failing to arrive on time

Missing bills and financial statements can be an indication of identity theft. Fraudsters might change the mailing address to hinder you from noticing unauthorized accounts or transactions. If you are not receiving your expected statements, contact your financial institutions immediately.

What to Do If You Suspect Credit Fraud

If you suspect credit fraud, it's essential to take quick and decisive action. Here's what you should do:

Notify your credit card issuer or bank

Report any unauthorized charges or suspected credit fraud to the financial institution involved. They will be able to assist you in resolving the issue, provide guidance, and if necessary, close or freeze the affected accounts.

Place a fraud alert on your credit report

Contact one of the three major credit bureaus (Experian, TransUnion, or Equifax) to place a fraud alert on your credit report. This alert will make it difficult for any fraudster to open new accounts in your name, as lenders and creditors will be required to verify your identity before extending credit.

File a police report and submit an identity theft affidavit

Filing a police report and submitting an identity theft affidavit provide official documentation that can be helpful in rectifying any credit report inaccuracies and disputing fraudulent charges or accounts. Additionally, it helps establish a paper trail that could aid in the apprehension of potential fraudsters.

Review and monitor your credit reports

Thoroughly review your credit reports for inaccuracies and unauthorized accounts. Continue to maintain vigilance and monitor your credit moving forward. Enlist the help of a credit monitoring service if necessary for added security.

Tips for Preventing Credit Fraud

Prevention is always better than cure. Here are some essential tips for safeguarding your credit against fraudsters:

Be cautious when sharing personal information, especially online or over the phone. Create strong, unique passwords for your online accounts, and update them regularly. Enable multi-factor authentication on financial accounts whenever possible. Secure your mail by using a locked mailbox and promptly collecting your mail each day. Shred sensitive documents (e.g., credit card statements, bank statements, tax documents) before discarding them to prevent theft.
In conclusion, recognizing credit fraud and being proactive in defending against it is critical in protecting your credit castle. By staying vigilant, monitoring your financial and credit activities, and taking swift action when you suspect fraud, you'll be empowered to maintain your hard-earned credit score and ensure long-term financial security.

10.2 Strategies against Identity Theft

In our increasingly connected world, identity theft has become one of the most significant threats to consumers' financial security. Developing effective strategies for protecting yourself against identity theft is critical for safeguarding your credit, and by extension, your financial future. This section will delve into several precautionary measures that you can implement to create a virtual fortress around your credit, keeping it secure from fraudsters and identity thieves.

Keep Your Personal Information Confidential

The first step in defending against identity theft is to keep your personal information confidential. Be cautious about disclosing sensitive information such as your Social Security number, date of birth, or bank account numbers, particularly online or over the phone. When transmitting personal data, always ensure that the recipient is a trusted entity and that the communication channel is secure.

Utilize Robust Security Measures

In our digital age, it's crucial to prioritize the security of your online presence. Invest in robust anti-virus and firewall protection for your devices, and always keep your software up to date. Regularly update your passwords, using a combination of upper and lowercase letters, numbers, and symbols to create a strong and unique password for each account. When possible, enable multi-factor authentication to provide an additional layer of security.

Secure Your Physical Documents

While the digital sphere is often the focus for security threats, it's essential not to neglect the protection of your physical documents. Invest in a fireproof safe to store essential documents such as your Social Security card, birth certificate, and tax records. Shred any financial statements, bills, or other sensitive documents that you no longer need to keep. By securing your physical documents, you minimize the risk of information falling into the wrong hands and prevent identity theft.

Monitor Your Credit Reports

One of the most effective tools for identifying identity theft early is to regularly monitor your credit reports. Check for any unfamiliar accounts or credit inquiries that may indicate fraudulent activity. In the United States, you are entitled to one free credit report per year from each of the three major credit bureaus, Experian, TransUnion, and Equifax. By staggering your requests, you can access a free report every four months, offering consistent insight into your credit standing throughout the year.

Limit Your Exposure to Phishing Scams

Phishing scams, where fraudsters attempt to obtain your personal information by posing as a legitimate entity, are a common method for identity theft. Vigilance is crucial in defending against these scams. Always be cautious when opening unfamiliar emails, clicking on links, or providing personal information to unverified sources. Only visit secure websites with an "https" URL and a padlock icon in the address bar.

Monitor Your Financial Accounts

Regularly checking your bank and credit card statements is a necessary step in maintaining your credit castle's security. Promptly report any unfamiliar transactions or unauthorized charges to your financial institution. By taking immediate action, you can often limit the damage caused by these fraudulent activities.

Respond Swiftly to Identity Theft

If you suspect that you have fallen victim to identity theft, it's essential to take swift and decisive action. Notify your bank and credit card issuers to halt any unauthorized transactions, place a fraud alert on your credit reports, and file a police report to document the crime. By acting quickly, you can minimize the potential damage and initiate the recovery process.

Educate Yourself on the Latest Scams and Threats

Identity thieves are becoming increasingly sophisticated, continually developing new methods to target their victims. Stay informed about the latest threats and scams by following reliable news sources and participating in online forums or community groups focused on financial security. By staying up-to-date on the latest tactics, you'll be better equipped to protect your credit castle from fraudsters.

In conclusion, the key to preventing identity theft lies in implementing effective strategies and maintaining vigilance over your credit and financial information. Building a robust defense around your credit castle by securing your personal information, utilizing strong security measures, and remaining educated about potential threats empowers you to maintain your hard-earned credit score and protect yourself from the devastating effects of identity theft.

10.3 Safeguarding Your Score from Unauthorized Inquiries

Unauthorized credit inquiries are a common pitfall in the quest to secure and maintain a strong credit score. These can occur due to the actions of unscrupulous individuals or institutions, making unsolicited checks into an individual's credit history. Such unauthorized access can have detrimental impacts on your credit score, and by extension, on your overall financial health. Hence, safeguarding your score from these unwelcome intrusions becomes not just sensible but paramount for your financial well-being.

Understanding Unauthorized Inquiries

Credit inquiries can be categorized as either 'soft' or 'hard' inquiries. Soft inquiries have no impact on your credit score and occur when you or a non-lending institution, like an employer or a rental company, checks your credit. A hard inquiry, on the other hand, requires your consent and is undertaken when a potential lender or a credit card company reviews your credit as part of a lending decision. These hard inquiries can marginally impact your credit score.

The danger lies when hard inquiries are made, without your approval or knowledge, and they begin to accumulate. This is what we term as 'unauthorized inquiries', a silent warning sign of unscrupulous activities or potential identity theft unfolding around your credit profile. These anonymous peeks into your credit history, when unchecked, could drive down your credit score without any fault of yours.

How To Detect Unauthorized Inquiries

The first step in safeguarding your score from unauthorized inquiries is efficient detection. An annual scan of your credit report could reveal unauthorized credit inquiries that you had no knowledge of. Remember, information is not just power; when we speak of credit scores, it becomes your shield.

Institutions like Experian, TransUnion, and Equifax in the US provide free annual credit reports. Investing your time to leaf through them allows you to spot unusual hard inquiries which you didn't consent to. Spotting them early enables you to tackle the issue head-on, thereby, limiting its impact on your credit score.

Disputing Unauthorized Inquiries

Once unauthorized inquiries are detected, the next pertinent step is to dispute them. Write directly to the credit bureau that reported the unauthorized hard inquiry with a formal letter describing your case.

In this letter, precisely mention the name of the institution that conducted the unauthorized check. Remember, your case becomes more substantial with the details. It's advisable to send these letters through certified mail with a return receipt. This will maintain a written record of your communication, key to demonstrating your proactive approach if disputes turn into legal confrontations.

A credit bureau typically takes between 30 to 45 days to investigate the claim. If the inquiry is ascertained to be unauthorized, it would be removed from your credit report, restoring your score points which were erroneously knocked off.

Your Role as a Credit-Informed Consumer

As one aspires to be a responsible credit consumer, we must understand that safeguarding yourself from unauthorized inquiries isn't just a one-off task. Rather, it should evolve into a habit that plays out in your financial decisions. Be cautious about who you share your confidential financial details with, and echo your explicit dissent if someone asks for your permission to undertake a hard credit inquiry without a legitimate reason.

Meanwhile, don't let the fear of unauthorized inquiries deter you from allowing necessary hard inquiries. Legitimate hard inquiries, resulting from a new loan or credit card application, are an expected part of your credit growth and shouldn't be seen as a toxic element to avoid. Instead, focus on managing the number of these inquiries within a short time, as a flurry of credit applications can portray you as someone dependent on credit, signaling red to potential lenders.

In conclusion, unauthorized inquiries can be a gnawing menace to your credit well-being, silently stealing credit points while you remain oblivious. The key to countering it lies not in some secret formula but lies in following the structured process of detection, dispute, and disciplined credit conduct. As you create your financial future, understanding these steps is not just vital but also empowers you to create a credit profile that unlocks the opportunities you aspire to.

10.4 The Role of Monitoring Services

In the captivating realm of credit scores, you are the grand architect of your financial present and future. Chapters of diligence, planning, strategy, and resolve define the book of your journey. But as you deftly navigate your course, crafting strategies, devising defenses, and daringly disputing unwarranted entries, consider this - would not your fortress benefit from a vigilant sentinel? A constant gaze to ensure that your diligently built credit repute isn't under silent attack? This is where credit monitoring services play their dedicated role in your voyage.

Unblinking Monitoring Eye

Picture a security system that watches your home around the clock, alerting you if a window is left unlocked, intruders attempt to break in, or a fire threatens your haven. This, essentially, is what a credit monitoring service does for your credit profile.

Credit monitoring is a service that tracks changes to your credit reports at one or more of the three major credit bureaus - Experian, TransUnion, and Equifax. It notifies you about any changes or suspicious activity within your credit report.

These services, like unceasing sentinels, keep a watchful eye on new credit inquiries, changes to credit limits, the opening of new credit accounts, delinquent payments, or public records like bankruptcies being linked to your account. By promptly alerting you of these changes, they allow you to rapidly respond to potential cases of identity theft or credit fraud, protecting your credit score from theft-inflicted damage.

Combatting Identity Theft

Identity theft is no minor menace; it's a monstrous hydra, rampantly rattling credit lives. Experian reported that as of 2020, around 14.4 million adults in the U.S. had become victims of identity fraud. A percentage of these attacks often spill into credit profiles, distorting scores, and spawning tumult in lives.

The Judicious use of credit monitoring services arms you against such threats. By immediately informing you of any new inquiries or accounts opened in your name that you haven't initiated, monitoring services provide an early identification mechanism against identity theft.

Meet Sara, a Queens-based accountant and a diligent custodian of her credit profile. She signed up for a credit monitoring service as she began to lean more on her credit potential to fortify her financial growth. One morning, Sara woke up to a notification about a new inquiry by a credit card provider - a card she hadn't applied for. Alarmed, she promptly reached out to the provider and had them freeze the account, stemming a potential identity theft at its root.

Navigating the Credit Sea

While safeguarding against threats and frauds is an essential part of a credit monitoring service, they also serve as useful navigation tools in your credit journey. Monitoring services, through regular credit reports and score updates, help you understand the impact of your financial actions on your credit score.

Looking to close a credit card account? Your monitoring service will help you understand how this could change your credit utilization rate and impact your score. Monitoring services' additional features, like identity theft protection, credit score simulators, and financial advice tailored to your credit status, could be the guiding lamps illuminating your credit path.

Choosing Your Sentry

As the value of credit monitoring services becomes more mainstream, the market for the same has broadened, offering a range of services to select from. While comparing features and pricing is essential, choosing a service that provides monitoring at all three major credit bureaus is advisable as it offers a well-rounded oversight of your credit profile.

Credit Salve, Not Scapegoat

While monitoring services play an essential role in fortifying your credit profile, lean not on them as crutches but as canes guiding your stride. These services do not directly improve or clean your credit reports; they are tools that provide rapid information and insight, empowering you to take appropriate action. The onus still lies on you to vigilantly manage your credit and proactively take steps towards credit score improvement while responding to instances of fraud and theft.

In our determined journey towards masterful credit stewardship, we must arm ourselves with all tools available. To craft a mold of robust credit strength that time, change, and financial demands cannot shatter, credibility monitoring services lend their unwavering gaze and guidance—your sentinels in the colossal credit castle that you erect. Above all else, remember, your credit future is yours to shape; monitoring services are but tools in your arsenal.

Chapter 11:
Sparkling Credit: Effective Credit Card & Loan Management

11.1 Credit Card Strategies for Better Scores

A Credit card whirls in a fascinating cycle around your credit score. It has the tantalizing power to fortify, fracture or reforge the pillars of your credit score, depending on how you wield it. As with any power, comes the onus to strategize, to plan, to wisely navigate the numerous features and potentials that credit cards flaunt. Embark on this endeavor with an open mind and a resolute will because the fruit of your journeys will be a shining credit score.

The Cardinal Rule: Regularity of Payments

Your payment history is the keystone in the architecture of your credit score. According to FICO, it constitutes a staggering 35% of your credit score. It's the primary lens through which lenders perceive your creditworthiness.

While it might seem like an obvious rule, it bears emphasis, all the same - always make your payments on time. Every missed payment is a hammer-strike on your credit score, and continuing this pattern can shatter your score to irreparable depths.

Take the story of Hannah, a science journalist from San Francisco. Hannah was making steady headway in her career but often made late credit card payments purely out of carelessness. Over a year, this created a scathing trail of late payments on her credit report, brutally eroding her credit score. Hannah decided to tackle the issue head-on, setting reminders and auto-payments, ensuring she never misses a payment deadline in the future.

However, all is not lost if you've missed payments in the past. Consistency in payments, even after past missteps, gradually but surely elevates your score. Let not past misses dishearten you, but instead inspire consistent timely payments henceforth.

So, find a stationery store, buy the biggest wall calendar you can find, mark your card payment dates in bold, red letters, put it up on your wall - and never miss another payment.

Maintain Low Credit Utilization

Credit Utilization, making up 30% of your credit score, is the second most vital facet impacting your score. This term involves the ratio between your debt and your available credit limit. Financial experts typically recommend maintaining a credit utilization rate of 30% or less.

Why does a high utilization rate potentially harm your credit score? Lenders see this as a sign of dependency on credit, which sparks fear of potential non-payment in the future in the lender's heart. It disconcerts lenders and sends a negative message about your capacity to manage finances.

So, if you have a credit card with a limit of, say, $10,000, try to maintain a balance lower than $3000. This practice communicates your ability to manage credit wisely and supports your quest towards a higher credit score.

Don't Rush to Close Old or Inactive Credit Cards

Hold onto your old credit cards for as long as you can. The age of credit plays a foundational role (15%) in determining your credit score. An older credit history communicates stability and longevity to lenders - highly desirable traits in a borrower.

On the same vein, inactive cards still contribute to your credit age and total credit limit, positively impacting your score. Before closing an unused card, consider the benefits it provides to your credit profile.

Keep Credit Applications to a Necessary Minimum

Each time you apply for a new credit, it triggers a 'hard inquiry' on your credit report. These inquiries indirectly herald potential risk to lenders and negatively impact your credit score. However, the impact of these inquiries is relatively minor and temporary.

An example might be Peter, a restaurant owner from Austin, who applied for multiple credit cards within a short time hoping to take advantage of their reward programs. These applications stack cumulatively on his credit report, resulting in a slight dip in his credit score. By minimizing new credit applications and spacing them wisely, Peter managed to regain his lost points and enhance his credit score over time.

A well-adjusted balance of restraint and wisdom is crucial in managing credit inquiries.

Leverage Reward Programs

Many credit cards offer valuable rewards to regular and prompt payers. These rewards can range from cash backs, points redeemable at specific vendors or services, airline miles, to discounts on a variety of purchases. While they don't directly impact your credit score, they can help offset some costs, making efficient management of credit more achievable.

To Conclude

Incorporating these strategies unfurls a fresh chapter in your credit journey, one replete with smart decisions, strategic planning, and score-boosting habits. Credit card is an effective tool in your credit enhancement arsenal. By understanding and using it well, you author your own tale of sparkling credit worthiness.

11.2 Wise Loan Management Practices

When we take a step back and observe, loans are indeed marvels of modern financing. They have the ability to unleash possibilities that would have been inaccessible otherwise due to financial constraints - be it a comfortable house, education at a prestigious institute, or the car you've had your eyes set on. Thanks to loans, dreams don't have to wait for the slow build-up of savings.

However, approaching loans with an uplifting spirit isn't enough. It requires the dedication of a craftsman, the mind of a chess player, and the heart of a marathon runner. The ability to strategize, plan ahead and sustain the path is crucial to stay ahead of the curve.

Embody the Attitude of a Paymaster

The credit world thrives on trust. As borrowers, we need to demonstrate that we are worthy of that trust. Regular repayments are symbolic of our commitment and reliability - they are the first step towards earning the lender's trust and boosting your credit score.

Take Anthony, a vigilant food truck owner from New York. Instilled with the ethos of discipline, Anthony set up an auto-debit system that deducted loan repayment amounts regularly from his account. He understood the core principle – to make timely repayments a N° 1 priority. Even during periods of financial strain, he adjusted other expenses, ensuring he never missed a loan payment.

Manifesting the attitude of a dutiful paymaster will guide you in your loan management endeavors.

Distinguish Between 'Need' and 'Want'

Smart loan management starts even before applying for the loan itself. It requires analyzing whether the loan you're considering is to cater to a 'need' or a 'want.' Needs are essentials - like a home or an education loan. Wants are driven by desires - a luxurious car or an extravagant vacation.

Samantha, a school teacher from Chicago, understood this distinction well. Even though passionate about travel, she suppressed the urge to apply for a travel loan for an enticing international vacation. She acknowledged that it would pile up unnecessary debt and put pressure on her financial stability if she couldn't keep up with the repayments.

Mastering the art of distinguishing between needs and wants places you on a firm footing on your loan management journey.

Embrace the Technique of Loan Consolidation

If you're shackled by multiple loans, loan consolidation can be a considerate ally. It combines your various loans into a single entity, ideally with a lower interest rate and longer repayment term. This streamlined process can make loan management more straightforward and efficient.

Marcus, a zealous entrepreneur from Los Angeles, was juggling various small business loans. He felt overwhelmed, trying to keep up with various interest rates and payment dates. By consolidating his loans, he relieved himself of undue pressure and replaced it with a better structure for managing his debt.

Applying loan consolidation wisely could pave the way for healthier loan management.

Explore the Potential of Refinancing

Refinancing is an opportunity to revisit the terms of your loan. This practice replaces your existing loan with a new one that ideally bears a lower interest rate. This change can help you save significant amounts over time.

Evelyn, who started as a sales executive in Boston, had initially taken out a student loan with a high-interest rate, due to her limited credit history. As her career took off, her income increased, and her credit score improved. Observing the positive shift in her financial situation, she decided to refinance her student loan. This move allowed her to reduce her interest rate, making her loan more manageable.

Refinancing, when used judiciously, offers a significant boost to your loan management strategy.

Guard Against Impulsive Borrowing

Loans offer tremendous potential, but they can be double-edged swords when wielded without caution. Impulsive borrowing can leave you handcuffed in a cycle of debt.

Consider Benjamin, an active social worker from Seattle. Despite their allure, he resisted payday loans to cope with a temporary crisis. He recognized the risk of impulsive borrowing and instead opted for a more sustainable strategy, trimming his monthly budget to weather the storm.

Avoiding impulsive borrowing forms the defensive shield of your loan management plan.

Charting Your Course to Financial Freedom

Loans, if managed wisely, can be launchpads to your dreams without becoming anchors weighing you down. The practices outlined above are not just strategies but life lessons - distinguishing needs from wants enhances decision-making, resisting impulsive borrowing nurtures financial self-control, loan consolidation encourages orderliness, and timely repayments honor self-discipline.

By espousing these practices, your voyage towards enhanced credit scores and financial liberation becomes a smoother sail.

11.3 Balance Transfers: Pros and Cons

Balance transfers may appear like enticing magic wands, promising to liberate you from spiraling credit card balances by bundling existing debt into a neat, manageable package. These financial tools enable you to move high-interest credit card debt onto a card with a considerably lower rate, often aided by an introductory zero-interest period. But is the magic they promise real or merely an illusion?

We must shed some light on this financial strategy's advantages and disadvantages to evaluate its actual potential. Our mission at hand is to grasp the essence of balance transfers and navigate this nebulous crossroad judiciously – whether they can be your loyal companions or turn into potential pitfalls.

Weighing the Advantages: Potential Boons of Balance Transfers

The Grace of Lower Interest Rates

The primary allure of balance transfers lies in the prospect of substantially lower interest rates. A balance transfer can be the bridge to freedom from burdensome credit card debts holding you in financial captivity. The key lies in the card offering an enticingly low-APR or even a zero-interest introductory period. Imagine the relief of seeing your mountainous high-interest debt diminish into smaller, more manageable molehills.

Take the case of Christine, a nurse in Miami, who was continually battling to downsize her credit card debt. Frustrated with exorbitant interest rates exacerbating her problem, she finally resorted to a balance transfer. To her surprise, the temporary zero-interest period allowed her to make sizeable dents in her debt without the menacing shadow of interest accumulation.

Streamlined Debt Management

At times, managing multiple credit cards might feel like a juggling act in a circus, where even a momentary lapse in concentration can invite disaster. Balance transfers introduce an element of simplicity. By consolidating debts onto a single card, you replace multiple payments with a singular monthly requirement— freeing mental space and reducing the risk of missed payments.

Consider the case of Kyle, an auto mechanic in Phoenix. Balancing various credit card repayments felt like a daunting task to him. After consolidating his debts through a balance transfer, his more streamlined financial landscape considerably eased his repayment stress.

Unveiling the Drawbacks: Hidden Traps of Balance Transfers

The Ominous Balance Transfer Fees

A not-so-obvious downside of balance transfers are the associated fees – typically around 3% - 5% of the amount transferred. Unknowing consumers might oversee these fees, believing in the imaginary magic of "free transfers." This fee can add a significant chunk to your debt, negating the savings made from reduced interest rates.

To put it into perspective, let's visit David, a school teacher from Detroit. Intrigued by the promise of a zero-interest period, he hastily opted for a balance transfer. However, he overlooked the 5% balance transfer fee, which unexpectedly inflated his debt and unraveled his repayment plans.

Lurking High APR After Introductory Period

The introductory lower interest rate that initially pulled you towards a balance transfer might not last indefinitely. After the grace period concludes, cardholders might find themselves facing APRs equal to or even more than what they had originally been trying to escape.

Reflect on Sarah, a restaurant owner from Houston. Her initial joy regarding her zero-interest balance transfer was short-lived when she was unable to pay off the balance within the introductory period. The subsequent spike in APR led to financial stress more severe than her initial problem.

Your Companion or Trap—What Will It Be?

Financial journeys often echo life's paradoxes. What seems like a boon might harbor hidden dangers and what first presents as a challenge could mask an opportunity. Balance transfers, too, embody this paradox. On one side, they hold the promise of lower interest rates and simplified debt management while on the flip side, they can deceive with balance transfer fees and lurking high APRs.

Navigating this paradox requires arming ourselves with knowledge, carefully analyzing the terms before riding the balance transfer wave. Like Austin, a firefighter from New York, who diligently compared balance transfer fees, post-introductory APRs, and his ability to clear the debt within the offer period. His thoughtful approach helped him maximize balance transfers' advantages while maneuvering around potential pitfalls.

For the pursuit of better credit score management and sparkling credit, understanding the pros and cons of balance transfers is fundamental.

11.4 Harnessing Reward Points

The landscape of credit card use is often dominated by discussions revolving around APRs, credit limits, and balance transfers. Yet this discourse sometimes sidelines a significant player that has been silently revolutionizing the credit card game – Reward Points. Astute consumers have discovered the potential buried beneath this perceived marketing gimmick and have been harnessing reward points to their advantage.

The Reward Points Phenomenon

Reward points are a token of appreciation that credit card companies offer their cardholders for every dollar spent. The accumulative value of these points can be redeemed in myriad ways – travel, merchandise, cash back, or even as payments towards your credit card bill. However, this seeming simplicity of reward points can often be shrouded in a smokescreen of terms and conditions, type of purchases, and redemption rules.

Jack, an IT professional from San Francisco, realized the power of reward points when he skillfully gathered points through his everyday transactions, eventually securing a free flight for his family vacation to Hawaii. All it took was a disciplined approach to swipe his rewards credit card for all his routine purchases and judicious management of his credit.

Planning for the Prize: Smart Strategies

To wield reward points powerfully, the journey begins with a plan. Consider your spending patterns, the categories where most of your expenses lie, and map these against the reward points on various credit cards. This thoughtful matching can help you peek into the future rewards that could be in store for you.

Let's visit a scenario from the life of Lisa, a fashion designer from Los Angeles. With a deep fascination for travel, she hunts for a card that offers generous rewards for purchases made in the travel category. Keeping this strategy in play, Lisa manages to earn significant points on hotel bookings and flights she would anyway have paid for. Lisa eventually finds herself basking in the sun on the sandy beaches of Malibu, thanks to the free flight she procured with her reward points.

The Dance Between Reward Points and Balances

A crucial aspect of garnering reward points is ensuring that the balance on your credit card does not grow out of control. The trick lies in using your credit card for planned purchases rather than impulse buys, and meticulously paying off your balance every month. This allows benefitting from reward points without falling into the entrapment of high-interest balances.

This strategy is beautifully illustrated in the life of Benjamin, a university professor from Chicago, who used his credit card for grocery shopping and bill payments, among other routine purchases. He made sure he settled his balance in full every month, avoiding the pitfall of inflated interest charges while reaping the reward points benefits.

The Labyrinth of Reward Terms

The prospect of reward points can seem less charming when caught in the labyrinth of terms and conditions. Many credit cards require a minimum spend amount for points to start accumulating and may even limit the maximum points that can be garnered in a specific period. Your dream of a free vacation can fizzle out if not watchful about redemption rules and expiry dates.

Take Melissa, an entrepreneur from Boston. She made extravagant purchases on her reward card, only to realize later that her card had a cap on the reward points that can be earned in a quarter. This understanding came a bit too late, resulting in a high credit balance without the imagined reward points to show for it.

Reward Points: A Financial Ally or Foil?

Like all elements of financial strategy, skillful handling of credit card reward points is a delicate dance between anticipation of benefits and mindful management of credit. Reward points can emerge as a silent ally, subtly cumulating into perceptible gains that can elegantly balance the scales of credit management.

Use your usual spending habits as a launchpad to extract maximum value from reward points. Through punctilious management of credit card balances and a fine understanding of reward terms, the potential of reward points can be harnessed, breathing a dash of sparkle in your journey towards a stellar credit.

Chapter 12:
Phoenix Rising: Rebuilding Credit after Bankruptcy & Financial Collapse

---

12.1 The Aftermath of Bankruptcy

Waking Up to a Financial Hangover

The weight of financial collapse is all too familiar to many, a crushing burden that can feel insurmountable. Declaring bankruptcy is akin to hitting the financial reset button, wiping out some, if not all, of your debts, but at a considerable cost. It may seem like a fresh start, but the harsh aftermath that follows is far from a stroll through a sunny meadow. From a shattered credit score to severely impaired borrowing power, the aftermath of bankruptcy is a rocky maze that must be tread with prudence and patience.

Bankruptcy Is Today, But Tomorrow is Another Day

Upon filing for bankruptcy, the sensation can be comparable to ripping off a band-aid – a brief moment of intense pain, followed by a feeling of relief. But the relief is temporary, eclipsed by the realization of a tarnished financial reputation. Unlike a simple band-aid, the financial wound of bankruptcy leaves behind a scar in the form of a chapter 7 bankruptcy record, lingering for up to 10 years on your credit report.

Not only are creditors less likely to lend to those considered high-risk, but denials can also become a common occurrence when applying for new lines of credit. The rosy credit card offers and loan approvals you once enjoyed now seem like a distant memory. Suddenly, your financial prospects appear grim, shackled by your past mistakes.

Take the case of Mike, a small business owner from Kansas. His once-thriving restaurant fell victim to the economic downturn, leaving him with crippling debt. Facing no other option, Mike filed for bankruptcy. He woke up the next day, staring at the mountain of repercussions, the cascade of financial consequences, the harsh reality of his newfound financial status.

The Credit Score Impact: A Plunging Free-Fall

One of the most significant repercussions of bankruptcy is the profound impact it has on your credit score. When Mike pulled his latest credit report, he nearly dropped his cup of coffee. From a credit score above 700, he saw his score had taken a nosedive, plunging down to the low 500's. This sharp decline is a common aftermath of bankruptcy, and it can be a chill-inducing sight for anyone in Mike's shoes.

Also, keep in mind that the impact on your credit score depends on where your score stands before bankruptcy. Those with higher credit scores may witness a more drastic drop than those already in the lower realms. It's a reality that often feels like salt in an open financial wound, provoking the burning question: How can I possibly recover from this?

Rebuilding Trust: The Power of Time

In the wake of bankruptcy, you may feel like a financial pariah. Lenders, once eager to extend credit, may now see you through wary lenses, scarred by the bankruptcy on your report. The truth is, bankruptcy inflicts damage on your image of reliability in the financial world. Despite this, there is room for recovery.

Charles, an aspiring home-owner from Pennsylvania, faced bankruptcy after being laid off unexpectedly from his long-time job. He grappled with debt, struggled to make ends meet, and was impacted severely by bankruptcy. But Charles did not let bankruptcy overshadow his dreams. More than anything else, he harnessed the power of time.

Bankruptcy is a red flag for lenders, but its impact wanes over time. Charles began rebuilding his reputation slowly and steadily. As each year passed, the weight of bankruptcy on his credit score became less severe, his financial decisions more refined, and his creditworthiness to lenders steadily improved. He knew regaining trust was more a marathon than a sprint.

A New Dawn: The Fresh Start You Need

Bankruptcy might entail a financial collapse, but it is not the end of the road. Consider it a stumble, a fall, but also a new beginning. Embrace the sobering aftermath of bankruptcy not as your downfall but as a fresh start. Remember - rising from bankruptcy is not impossible; it's a challenge that requires commitment, resilience, and time.

12.2 Rebuilding Strategy Post-Bankruptcy

Bankruptcy—an intense financial wildfire—can feel like it chars all it touches, leaving a bleak landscape in its wake. However, have you noticed how nature convinces life to sprout and sprig from the seemingly doom-laden ashes? Bankruptcies work the same way. Yes, they wound, but they also pave the way for a stronger, more resilient, and knowledgeable you.

Post-bankruptcy credit rebuilding is your personal phoenix moment, an opportunity to rise from the ashes of financial turmoil, stronger and brighter. Let's dive into the key strategies that can assist you in this journey.

Rebuilding Credit Timeline

- Continue disputes
- Open secured card
- Make on-time payments

- Continue disputes
- Open secured card
- Make on-time payments

Month 1 Month 2 Month 3 Month 4 Month 5 Month 6 Month 7 Month 8 Month 9 Month 10 Month 11 Month 12

- Obtain credit reports
- Identify inaccuracies
- Dispute errors

- Apply for credit builder loan
- Maintain low credit utilization

- Check credit score
- Set new financial goals

Patience and diligence in making on-time payments leads to credit rebuilding success

Embrace the Second Chances

Bankruptcy may flicker as a glaring red on your financial report, but remember—it's not inscribed in stone. The aftereffects corrode away with time, and lenders recognize this. The key is to understand that bankruptcy signals a fresh start, not a permanent setback.

Lynn, a single mother from Chicago, found herself grappling with debilitating debt following an unexpected illness. With mounting medical bills, Lynn had no choice but to embrace bankruptcy. Accepting bankruptcy wasn't giving in—it was an acknowledgment of her present circumstances, a brave first step toward regaining control.

Understanding the Secured Route

In a world where unsecured credit seems challenging, turning to secured credit cards can be an effective strategy. A secured credit card, backed by a cash deposit acting as collateral, can provide a means to begin rebuilding credit history.

An architect from New York, Howard, found himself rebuilding his life after bankruptcy. Shut out from most traditional lines of credit, Howard opted for a secured credit card. This approach worked as the cornerstone to Howard's credit rebuilding strategy, allowing him to start constructing his financial future.

Avoiding the Deception of Subprime Credit Cards

Subprime credit cards, with their promise of quick approvals, may appear as an alluring oasis in your post-bankruptcy financial desert. However, this oasis often turns out to be a mirage, laden with high interest rates and mountainous fees.

Jennifer, a schoolteacher from Portland, had experienced bankruptcy, following her divorce. Pelted with subprime credit card offers, she felt tempted to grab what felt like low-hanging fruit. But a closer look unveiled their hidden perils. High fees, astronomical APRs, uncapped late fees—all hiding in the fine print, ready to trip the unwary.

Emphasizing on Timely Payments — Size Doesn't Matter

Payment history trumps all when it comes to credit scores, contributing up to 35% of your FICO score, the largest chunk. Your finances might require down-sizing post-bankruptcy, but resistance to slipping into late payments is crucial.

Consider the example of Brad. He faced bankruptcy due to his construction business's downturn, which forced him to readjust his entire financial scenario. For Brad, every payment mattered, as he realized on-time payments—big or small—were the keys to gradually restore his credit standing.

Budget Planning - Essential Armor in the Financial Battlefield
In the journey toward credit rebuilding, budgeting proves an essential tool, acting as your discerning night-vision goggles in the darkened alleys of post-bankruptcy finances.

Take Sandra, for instance, a florist from Miami, who combated her post-bankruptcy blues with a detailed budget. Penning down her monthly income and expenses, Sandra gained a clear vision of her financial standpoint and could set achievable goals to pay off debts, contribute to savings and, slowly but steadily, rebuild her credit.

Gaining from Credit Counseling

Post-bankruptcy, credit counseling can be a wave of guidance in the turbulent seas of financial struggle. Non-profit credit counseling organizations can provide the necessary education and guidance to manage personal finances better and navigate the credit rebuilding process.

Sam, a car mechanic from Atlanta, felt lost in the financial maze following his bankruptcy. A credit counseling agency became his beacon, illuminating the path towards a sound financial standing.

Be Patient - The Clock is Your Ally

Remember, credit rebuilding isn't a sprint—it's a marathon. Patience, therefore, might just be your most valuable ally, allowing the shadows of bankruptcy to fade, and your creditworthiness to resurface in the warm sunshine of financial recuperation.

For every phoenix—every Lynn, Howard, Jennifer, Brad, Sandra, and Sam—the story began amidst daunting challenges. But these very challenges forged the bedrock for their rise to financial recovery. Each battle fought left them stronger, more equipped, and inching closer towards their goal – a triumphant resurgence from bankruptcy.

12.3 Financial Management to Avoid Future Collapse

In the wake of a financial crisis, such as bankruptcy, it is crucial to re-emerge with the wisdom to prevent a repeat event. It may seem as if the task is akin to Sisyphus pushing his boulder up the hill only to watch it fall back again. Nonetheless, just like the mythic hero found worth in his endless struggle, so can bankruptcy survivors find value in their journey to financial stability. This chapter aims to provide hands-on guidance and introduce the tools to ensure lasting financial health by careful financial management.

An Epic Journey Starts With a Single Step: The Urgency of A Change

Commonly, our financial decisions are based on habits rather than conscious choices. The unfortunate collapse can serve as a wake-up call, giving you the power to rewrite your financial story. Let's consider Travis, a tech entrepreneur from San Francisco. After his start-up failed, he was crushed by debt. But the painful experience gave him an urgency to change his financial habits. Rather than drifting through reactive decision-making, he became proactive, delving into budgets, and developing smart savings plans to avoid future collapses.

From Chaos to Order: The Power of Budgeting

Establishing a detailed and realistic budget is akin to laying a foundation for a house. Without it, the structure becomes shaky and could collapse at any minor shakeup in the economic landscape. Anne, a marketing specialist in Texas, endured bankruptcy following a period of excessive spending. Learning from her turmoil, Anne sought refuge in budgeting. Pained by the recurring nightmares of her fiscal past, she painstakingly recorded her monthly income and expenses, developing a granular understanding of her fiscal conditions. As a result, she safeguarded herself from future financial collapses, showcasing the power of budgeting.

Lifeboats for Future Storms: The Vitality of Emergency Savings

An emergency fund is the key lifeboat that sails you through unexpected situations. Allocating money monthly to this fund can mitigate the effects of sudden financial storms like job loss, medical bills, or urgent car repairs. For example, Walter, a restaurateur from Boston, was forced into bankruptcy when his restaurant was damaged in a fire. In his journey to financial recovery, Walter prioritized building an emergency savings fund to handle potential future disasters, providing him with a sense of security and control.

Financial Literacy: The Map and Compass to Navigate the Fiscal Landscape

One cannot stress enough the importance of financial literacy. By understanding the fundamentals of finance, individuals can make informed decisions and avoid fiscal pitfalls. Madeline, a nurse in Denver, was declared bankrupt due to her inability to understand her home loan conditions. Determined to prevent a relapse, she educated herself in finance, gaining invaluable knowledge about loans, credit scores, and interest rates. The enhanced understanding of the financial landscape provided her with a compass to navigate successfully and avoid future financial collapses.

Every Penny Counts: The Strategy of Downscaling

Downscaling or learning to live within one's means can be pivotal in the journey towards financial health. It may require making tough choices, but eventually, it fosters a resilient fiscal approach. Consider David, a real estate agent in Miami, declared bankrupt due to his extravagant lifestyle. On his road to recovery, David recognized the profound value of money. Instead of taking on overwhelming mortgages for his sea-view apartment, he downscaled and lived in a budget-friendly home, freeing resources to build a sturdy financial structure.

Watching the Signs: Staying Alert to Changes

Changes often act as a barometer of the financial environment. Staying attuned to these changes can function as a forward-warning system, allowing preventive action. Brenda, a freelance writer in New York, faced bankruptcy when print magazines saw a slump. This time, she was alert to the winds of change. As digital media started gaining traction, Brenda swiftly shifted gears, protecting herself from another financial collapse.

In conclusion, future financial collapses can be triumphantly avoided by implementing strategic preventative measures. The lessons shared in this chapter provide you with the necessary sails to weather the stormy seas of bankruptcy and emerge stronger.

12.4 Case Studies: Recovery through Strategic Planning

In the realm of finances, a major setback such as bankruptcy or financial collapse can shatter confidence and breed despair, mirroring a boxer knocked down in the ring with a dazed vision and scrambled senses. Yet, the story isn't about the knockout blow; rather, it's about the arduous journey back to one's feet. A look into the real-life episodes of financial resurrections serves as a beacon of hope for beckoning comeback journeys. They showcase how strategic planning catapulted them from the depths of despair to soaring heights of financial freedom.

Jillian's Story: The Phoenix of Patient Care

Meet Jillian, a registered nurse in Philadelphia whose life took a drastic turn when she faced bankruptcy. Jillian had always been enthusiastic about providing healthcare services to the needy but failed to manage her own financial health. Overwhelmed by student loans, mortgage payments, and credit card debt, her world crumbled when she was forced to declare bankruptcy.

Amid financial ashes, however, emerged Jillian's phoenix: the commitment to strategically plan her financial recovery. She resolved to take control of her financial narrative and curtail her spending, recognizing the urgency to break free from the encircling pitfalls of unnecessary expenditure.

Jillian's first step was to establish a practically limiting budget to guide her spending habits. This was not an easy feat, as it required significant lifestyle changes. But determination fuelling her, she marked out her expenses, cutting out luxuries until her financial position improved. Slowly but surely, she managed to fit her life into the tight boundaries of her new budget.

Her momentous journey didn't stop at frugality. Jillian was mindful that fully overcoming bankruptcy required building healthy credit. She tiptoed back into the credit world, cautiously taking on credit she could afford while ensuring prompt payment. She recognized the importance of having a devisor to guide her actions for the better; hence a credit coach became her financial guru, helping her to rebuild her credit score over time.

Jillian's tale is a testament to the power of recovery through careful, strategic planning. It personifies the very essence of a phoenix, embodying the concept of emerging stronger from adversity.

Benjamin's Narrative: The Comeback Kid of Coding

The tech industry appears glamorous, but it's notoriously unpredictable. Benjamin, a software developer from San Diego, learned it the hard way. His dream to run a startup soon turned into a nightmare, pushing him to financial collapse when the startup failed to gain traction.

Devastated but resilient, Benjamin began his journey back to financial stability, underlining the importance of strategic planning. He carefully pivoted his career, shifting from an independent startup owner to providing freelance projects. This new approach provided a steady income stream, the foundation of his recovery.

Simultaneously, Benjamin recognized the importance of savings in preventing future financial collapse. He made a solemn commitment to save a portion of his earnings regularly, acting as a cushion against unforeseen financial crises. He also began to meticulously analyze his spending patterns, prioritizing necessary expenses over luxuries.

Benjamin's rebound was steeped in financial literacy. Like a proactive scholar, he delved into understanding financial concepts, investing his time in learning about interest rates, credit scores, and the dynamics of lending institutions. Such dedicated learning empowered him to make well-informed choices, further consolidating his financial recovery plan.

His journey is an illustration of what strategic planning coupled with strong willpower can achieve, brilliantly exemplifying a well-planned comeback.

Reflections

These stories serve not just as words of encouragement. They also provide practical steps for anyone navigating the difficult path of financial recovery. Jillian and Benjamin's stories provide valuable insights into the critical factors of recovery. These include disciplined budgeting, strategic credit-managing, gaining financial literacy, and developing consistent savings habits. These strategies offer a roadmap, leading one from financial collapse to recovery. As each person's situation is unique, the key is to adapt these learnings into a personalized recovery strategy.

Remember that every crisis permits a fresh start, a chance to rewrite your financial narrative differently. The crunch of financial collapse, though painful, provides the opportunity to build stronger monetary practices.

Chapter 13:
Credit Maintenance for Life: Establishing Long-Term Financial Health

13.1 Check and Repeat: Regular Credit Checkups

Just like we attend regular medical checkups to ensure our bodies are healthy and catch potential problems early, our financial well-being necessitates a similar approach - regular credit checkups. Keeping tabs on your credit health is a crucial element in the pursuit of long-term financial stability. This simple, yet often overlooked practice provides a holistic view of your credit health, enabling you to take timely corrective actions as needed.

The Power of Tracking: Maintaining an Accurate Credit Pulse

Consistently monitoring your credit score and report reinforces awareness of your financial landscape, empowering you to make informed decisions for a healthy credit profile. Track your credit diligently, not only to identify potential errors but also to comprehend how different factors weigh on your score, such as credit utilization, payment history, and inquiries. This heightened understanding acts as your compass, guiding you to make strategic credit-related decisions.

Performing these credit checkups at regular intervals (ideally, at least once a quarter) allows you to prevent surprises and adapt your financial strategy. Monitoring your credit score frequently also helps ensure the information on your credit report is accurate and up-to-date. As a result, you can address inaccuracies that may adversely impact your score before they escalate into bigger issues.

Fighting Fraud: Identifying Identity Theft & Unauthorized Activity

Credit report monitoring doubles as an essential line of defense against identity theft and fraud. One of the earliest signs of such unauthorized activity lies hidden in your credit report. Keeping an eagle eye on your report enables prompt detection of fraudulent accounts, loans, or credit inquiries made under your name, safeguarding your financial fortress from malicious attacks.

By taking a proactive stance in combatting fraud, you can initiate corrective measures, such as freezing your credit, filing disputes, or placing fraud alerts with credit bureaus early on.

Nipping these issues in the bud is crucial to protect your hard-earned credit score from the ramifications of illicit activity.

Navigating the Roadmap: Your Credit Report as a Guide

Regular credit checkups can uncover trends or patterns that may warrant attention or modification in your financial behavior. For instance, suppose your report consistently highlights a high credit utilization rate. In that case, it signals the need to adopt a strategy to better manage debt, such as paying off balances promptly or applying for a higher credit limit. Identifying these trends early enables you to pivot your financial strategy, bolstering your credit profile over time.

Comparing the snapshot of your credit report against your personal financial goals and milestones can also be a potent motivator, spurring you to course-correct and remain disciplined in your financial journey.

A Confidence Catalyst: The Psychological Benefits of Credit Monitoring

Monitoring your credit health frequently promotes a more positive relationship with your finances, further setting you up for long-term success. Watching your credit score improve over time, as a result of diligent financial management, can foster a heightened sense of confidence and self-efficacy, spurring you on to stay on your path to financial freedom.

On the flip side, witnessing a dip in your credit score might trigger emotions of frustration or disappointment, leading to meaningful reflection on any missteps. Ultimately, the power of tracking your credit performance rests in the issuance of a reality check, nudging you to stay accountable to your financial goals.

Embracing Technology: Your Credit Monitoring Ally

Leverage the wealth of tools and technology available to simplify credit monitoring. Many credit monitoring services and financial tools provide free access to your credit scores, alerting you to significant changes. These technological allies eliminate any barriers (like fees or inconvenience) that may hinder regular credit checkups, allowing for seamless credit tracking.

Embrace regular credit checkups as a deliberate and proactive approach to managing your financial health. By doing so, you cultivate a proactive, conscientious outlook that underscores long-term financial stability. Your credit report serves as the mirror reflecting your financial decisions – dare to look into it often, armed with the knowledge and determination to improve your financial outlook.

13.2 The Importance of Stable Financial Habits

Regaining control over financial health and fostering resilience against financial instability necessitates more than just understanding credit concepts and strategic applications. It demands adopting a thorough, deep-rooted change that starts with restructuring our financial habits from the ground up. As Benjamin Franklin astutely observed, "Your net worth to the world is usually determined by what remains after your bad habits are subtracted from your good ones." This principle holds particularly true when it comes to maintaining a sustainable and healthy credit score.

Laying Down the Foundation: Stable Financial Habits

Stable financial habits are the building blocks that lay the foundation for credit maintenance and financial freedom. They pertain to the day-to-day actions we take regarding our financial decisions, such as adhering to a budget, timely bill payments, and conscious spending. These habits, when consistently practiced, garner influential power over our financial wellbeing and mold our credit health's trajectory.

The adherence to stable financial habits fosters discipline and allows us to maintain control over our financial lives. By equipping ourselves with the power to make sound financial decisions regularly, we author our own financial health narrative and shape the course of our financial future. Each consistent habit works in unison towards constructing a fortress of financial stability, one that provides a strong defense against bouts of financial instability and shields our credit score.

Financial Stability: The Birthplace of Impressive Credit Scores

An unwavering commitment to stable financial habits has a direct, positive impact on credit scores. Consistent and timely payments evidence reliability, cutting down on the credit risk perceived by lenders, laying the groundwork for higher credit ratings. Keeping credit usage within recommended limits demonstrates financial prudence, adding favorably to part of the credit score determination formula. Supplementally, by keeping old accounts open and diversifying your credit types, you display adept credit management skills, contributing to longevity and diversity factors considered in calculating credit scores.

The gradual, uphill rise in credit scores, born out of the dedication to stable financial habits, in turn, usher in multiple perks. From qualifying for lower interest rates on loans, securing approvals for higher credit limits to enjoying bargaining leverage, the rewards for good credit scores are ample, planting the seeds for future financial prosperity.

A Safety Net Against Financial Turbulence

Stable financial habits function as a safety net against financial uncertainties and unforeseen crises. A practiced habit of saving, for instance, ensures the ready availability of an emergency fund to weather any financial storms without resorting to credit or loans, thus preserving your credit score.

Additionally, when we establish good financial habits, such as limiting unnecessary expenses or avoiding impulsive purchases, we position ourselves to better navigate fiscal turbulence. The financial discipline ingrained through these habits acts as a compass during crises, guiding you to make decisions that ensure your credit score remains unscathed amid chaos.

Paving the Path towards Financial Freedom

Just as poor habits can precipitate a cycle of bad credit and financial hardship, good financial habits can stimulate a cycle of wealth creation and security. The routine act of regularly contributing to a retirement fund or investment portfolio can exponentially grow your wealth over time, establishing long-term financial security. Similarly, the habit of monitoring your credit report allows for swift detection and correction of any errors or fraudulent activity, providing essential protection to your credit history and score.

Importantly, the commitment to good financial habits extends beyond your individual financial wellness. It also plays a crucial role in shaping the financial mindset of future generations. Children who grow up witnessing their parents practice good financial habits are likely to apply these same habits in adulthood, proliferating financial literacy and prosperity.

Financial stability is not a destination, but a journey, one that demands dedication and consistency. Just as regular exercise and healthy eating habits are essential for physical well-being, stable financial habits are indispensable for maintaining credit health and achieving financial freedom.

13.3 Long-term Goal Setting for Successful Credit Maintenance
Understanding the Pertinence of Long-term Goals

Credit maintenance for life is not a sprint; it's a marathon. It's not just about achieving a desired credit score, but consistently retaining it over the years. Decoding this journey's secret entails understanding the profound merits of long-term goal setting. Prioritizing the immediate need to improve our credit score is essential, but charting out a long-term course will empower you to retain and enhance this score over time.

Ralph Waldo Emerson once noted, "the only person you are destined to become is the person you decide to be." When it comes to credit maintenance, the decision to not only be, but remain a person with a healthy credit score, demands the establishment of long-term financial goals. These goals serve as your North Star, illuminating your path, guiding your actions, and keeping your financial habits in check.

Mapping Financial Destinations

Long-term goals can be viewed as mapping your financial destinations. Imagine planning a cross-country road trip—the final destination is crucial, but so too are the pit stops, the travel speed, the refueling and maintenance necessary to travel the entire distance. Much like a comprehensive road trip plan, outlining long-term financial goals provides a detailed route towards optimal credit maintenance. It pinpoints the key actions that need to be taken, the habits that need to be instilled, and the financial milestones to be achieved to reach your ultimate credit destination.

For instance, a young adult aiming to purchase their dream home within the next ten years can establish specific long-term financial goals like maintaining a credit utilization ratio below 30%, keeping up timely bill payments, exploring diverse credit types, and continuously monitoring their credit report, among others. These long-term goals, when pursued consistently, inch them closer to their dream house while strengthening their overall credit health for the future.

Fostering Financial Discipline and Perseverance

Beyond acting as financial roadmaps, long-term goals foster a sense of discipline and perseverance crucial for successful credit maintenance. The journey to your perfect credit score isn't always smooth—it can stumble upon financial potholes and cross unforeseen detours. By having well-established long-term goals, we are conditioned to stay committed to our financial course, regardless of the challenges that might arise.

Defining long-term goals instills a perspective that sees beyond temporary setbacks. It empowers individuals to bounce back from minor financial missteps with minimal impact on their overall credit journey. Additionally, long-term goals bolster financial discipline as they consistently reinforce the importance of sound financial decisions and the stakes tied to them.

The Power of Purposeful Action

With long-term goals in place, every financial action becomes purposeful and effective. The act of repaying a loan installment or avoiding impulsive splurges isn't merely seen as a recurrent task but as a purposeful stride taken to achieve the defined financial goal. This sense of purpose, imbued in every financial choice, amplifies savings efforts, discourages inappropriate spending, and betters credit profile management.

Facilitating Continuous Financial Growth

Long-term goal setting also facilitates continuous financial growth, essential for lifelong credit maintenance. Setting and achieving one long-term goal often sets the stage for the next, fostering a cycle of consistent credit improvement and financial prosperity. For example, a person who has accomplished their financial goal of entering the realm of 700+ credit scores can set a new objective—like reaching an 800+ score within the next five years. The ripple effect of long-term goal setting keeps you in constant pursuit of better credit health, securing your financial future.

Establishing long-term financial goals is, therefore, not an option, but a necessity for successful credit maintenance. It paves the path to financial stability, instills sound credit habits, and fuels the pursuit of an exemplary credit score. It's akin to investing in a lifeline that safeguards your credit health amidst the waves of financial unpredictability and turbulence.

13.4 Leveraging Tools & Technology for Credit Health
The Digital Age of Financial Management

In our ever-advancing world, technology has weaved itself into every aspect of our lives – and our finances are no exception. As we traverse the path to long-term financial health and exceptional credit scores, it is essential to leverage the vast array of tools and technology available to make the journey smoother, more efficient, and ultimately more successful. By strategically utilizing digital resources, we can monitor our credit health, better understand the factors influencing our credit score, and easily track progress towards our financial goals.

Let's explore some of the game-changing tools and technologies available and learn how to harness their power to cultivate stable financial habits and facilitate credit maintenance for life.

Credit Monitoring Services: Your Financial Watchdog

Regular credit checkups are crucial for maintaining optimal credit health. Thanks to the plethora of credit monitoring services available, keeping a watchful eye on our credit profiles has never been easier. These services serve as our financial watchdog, alerting us to changes in our credit score, flagging potential issues, and providing key insights into our credit health.

Some popular and widely-used credit monitoring services include Credit Karma, Experian, myFICO, and TransUnion. Many of these platforms offer free services with the option to upgrade to premium accounts for more advanced features and personalized recommendations. By regularly using these services, we build a strong foundation for long-term financial health by keeping ourselves informed and empowered.

Understanding the Impact: Credit Score Simulators

We often find ourselves wondering: "What would happen if...?" Credit score simulators are an innovative solution to answer these questions without the need for costly experiments. With simulators, like those offered by Credit Karma and myFICO, we can input hypothetical financial scenarios to predict their potential impact on our credit score. This can include changes such as opening a new credit card, paying off debt, or having a late payment.

Credit score simulators help us make well-informed and responsible financial decisions without facing the real-world consequences. As we progress on our financial journey, these insights can prove invaluable, enabling us to develop a deeper understanding of how our actions affect our credit health and implement the best strategies for success.

Building Good Habits: Expense and Budget Trackers

One of the most vital aspects of credit maintenance is developing and adhering to a budget that reflects our financial goals. This is where expense and budget trackers come into play. Apps such as You Need a Budget (YNAB), Mint, and Wally can aid us in creating customized budgets, tracking our expenses, and warning us when we've strayed from our financial path.

The power of these tools lies in their ability to effectively bridge the gap between our daily spending habits and our long-term financial objectives. By using expense and budget trackers consistently, we can reinforce our commitment to cultivating credit-boosting habits and monitor our progress towards achieving our financial dreams.

Harnessing Data: Personalized Financial Advice

Imagine having a personal financial advisor who understands our individual needs and offers tailored recommendations based on our financial situation. With AI-powered fintech platforms, this is now possible. Platforms like Wallet.ai use artificial intelligence and machine learning algorithms to analyze our financial data and provide guidance to optimize our financial decisions further.

By leveraging these advanced technologies, we can gain valuable insights and practical advice to make smarter financial choices, all the while maintaining our credit health and fostering habits that ensure long-term financial success.

Empowering Security: Identity Theft Protection

As we become increasingly reliant on digital tools, it is crucial to protect our financial information from potential threats. Identity theft protection services such as LifeLock and IdentityForce can be our first line of defense against credit-related fraud, helping to secure our credit scores and maintain our hard-earned financial stability.

These services monitor suspicious activities on our credit profiles and alert us to potential threats, giving us peace of mind and allowing us to focus on growing our credit with confidence.

In conclusion, today's technology offers us a wealth of tools and resources designed to support and elevate our financial journey. By actively leveraging the advantages provided by credit monitoring services, score simulators, expense and budget trackers, AI-driven fintech platforms, and identity theft protection, we can keep our financial goals within reach and establish long-term credit health. As we embrace these innovations, we will find ourselves empowered, informed, and equipped to master our financial destiny.

Chapter 14:
Mastering the Credit Universe: Expert-Level Strategies & Tips

14.1 Advanced Tactics for an Impressive Credit Score
A Symphony of Sound Strategies

Mastering the credit universe goes beyond understanding fundamental elements and maintaining consistency. It involves embracing and implementing advanced strategies that not only build an admirable credit score but also maintain it with finesse. Your pursuit of an impressive credit score is akin to an aspiring maestro mastering Chopin's complex compositions. It's about hitting the right notes, at the right times, and in the right sequence. The strategies discussed will shine a light on some of the more refined techniques that will help you play a breathtaking financial symphony.

Diversifying Your Credit Mix

In the world of finance, diversification is a strategy primarily employed to spread out risk. This concept is not limited to investments alone; it extends to your credit profile as well. Just as a maestro uses a variety of instruments to create a rich symphony, diversifying your credit mix—ensuring you have a blend of installment loans (like mortgages and student loans) and revolving credit (like credit cards)—adds depth to your credit history. This assortment not only demonstrates your ability to handle different types of credit but also has the potential to boost your credit score.

It's vital, though, to approach this strategy thoughtfully. Acquiring different types of credit should be an organic process driven by your financial needs and not solely by the goal of diversifying your credit.

Maximizing the Credit Utilization Strategy

Every maestro has a set of key notes they lean on to create their masterpiece. In the credit score symphony, one of those key notes is credit utilization. It accounts for approximately 30% of a FICO score, making it one of the top factors influencing your credit rating.

Credit utilization is the ratio of your credit card balances to your total credit limits. An ideal ratio is generally around 30%, but if we're talking about expert-level strategies, keeping it at

10% or lower can offer additional benefits. It reflects positively on your credit profile, showing lenders that you can manage credit responsibly and not overextending yourself.

Strategic Credit Card Applications

Oftentimes, a maestro will introduce a new instrument into the ensemble to add a unique layer to the performance. Similarly, strategically applying for new credit cards can enhance your credit score performance.

However, it is important to note that applying for multiple credit cards recklessly can harm your credit score. How then can you apply this strategy effectively? Timing is crucial. When you apply for new credit cards strategically—say, when you are planning a big purchase or you've paid off a sizeable debt—you can possibly get lower interest rates or take advantage of enticing reward programs.

Note, though, that each credit card application could cause a temporary dip in your credit score due to the hard inquiry on your credit report. However, if you plan and time everything carefully, your score should rebound, and you'll be conducting even richer harmonies in due time.

Mindful of Older Accounts

Some of the most heartfelt symphonies gain depth and resonance through the song's older, deeper notes. A similar principle applies to credit history. Older accounts are those deeper notes in your credit score symphony, providing a sense of history and stability to your overall financial profile.

Sometimes, it may be tempting to close an old, unused account. But before you do, consider how it could affect your credit score. Older credit accounts help lengthen your credit history, which is a positive factor in your credit score calculation. It shows lenders that you have a long track record of credit use.

These advanced tactics can help you earn an impressive credit score, but they require a mindful, strategic approach coupled with a profound understanding of the credit universe's nuances. Just like how a maestro blends unique notes together to create a moving, unforgettable masterpiece, mixing these strategies will enable you to conduct an impressive credit score performance.

As we navigate this promising journey together, remember the power of persistence, strategy, and knowledge, and keep playing your credit score symphony until it resonates impressively across the financial universe.

14.2 When to Leverage Credit and When to Avoid

The Two Faces of Credit

Credit, a powerful financial tool, can play dual roles in our lives. At times, it emerges as a steadfast ally, bolstering financial stability and fostering growth. However, mishandled, it can transform into a troublesome adversary leading you down a daunting path of escalating debts and financial catastrophe. Mastering the art of leveraging credit and discerning when to avoid it, is akin to becoming a seasoned sailor capable of taming even the wildest financial storms.

The Art of Leveraging Credit

Think of credit as a rickety suspension bridge that spans a vast chasm. Navigating it with a light, balanced load (minimal, manageable debt) and taking steps only when certain (strategically timed credit utilization) is the path to safety. Conversely, sprinting across with a heavy load (excessive debt) or in foggy conditions (uncertain financial times) can result in a precarious wobble, or worse yet, a tumble into the chasm.

Empowering Dreams: Credit as Your Ladder to Success

Credit, when leveraged mindfully, can be a wonderful ally in empowering your dreams. Consider a tale of two aspiring homeowners - Alice and Bob. Both are keen on purchasing their first homes. Alice, with a respectable credit score under her belt, has access to mortgages at more favorable rates. On the other hand, Bob, burdened by a poor score, struggles with loan approvals and is offered significantly higher interest rates. With her leveraged credit, Alice not only fulfills her dream of homeownership, but does so affordably, freeing up her financial resources for other goals.

Bouncing Back: Strategic Credit Use Post Financial Setbacks

Credit can also be a resourceful companion during life's unpredictable setbacks. Imagine there's John, a middle-aged professional who recently lost his job. Although he has some savings set aside, he strategically uses credit to maintain his lifestyle while seeking out employment. This tactic allows him to draw out his savings over a more extended period and provides a safety cushion.

It's crucial to remember that strategic leveraging of credit within manageable limits is key here. It's about using credit to bolster financial flexibility without sinking deep into unwieldy, long-term debt.

Beware the Pitfalls: When to Steer Clear of Credit

While properly managed credit can undeniably be a robust financial tool, there are instances when it's best to avoid its lure and instead rely on financial discipline and patience.

The Tides of Financial Stability: Spending Within Your Means

Consider Emily, an enthusiastic shopper charmed by the mirage of limitless spending power offered by her heap of credit cards. She splurges frequently, unconcerned about the accumulating balances on her cards. When the dues pile high, she barely manages to scrape through the minimum payments, resulting in a spiraling vortex of escalating debts, interest charges, and plunging credit scores.

Emily's tale is a stark reminder that although credit can provide the illusion of increased spending power, it is, in fact, borrowed money. It's vital to live within your means and resist the temptation of discretionary spending via credit, which only amounts to escalating debts.

Your Financial Scorecard: Protect Your Credit Health

Another scenario when you should sidestep credit is when your credit health is hanging in the balance, and any negative interaction can cause it to topple. Suppose you're on the verge of crossing your credit utilization ratio or recently faced multiple hard inquiries. Here, any further applications for credit, even if approved, can place additional strain on your credit score.

Avoiding credit in these instances might require high levels of discipline and patience, but the leg up it imparts to your credit score recovery is well worth it.

Mastering the delicate dance with credit — knowing when to waltz forward and leverage it and recognizing when to step back and avoid it — is an instrumental step towards establishing enduring financial stability and credit health. This dance, however, is not just a choreographed routine; it requires you to tune in to your individual financial melody, understand the rhythm of your income streams, and dance in harmony with your financial aspirations.

14.3 Expert Tips for Managing Multiple Credit Lines

The beauty of a kaleidoscope is derived from its multitude of shimmering fragments assembled ingeniously into a dazzling whole. Managing multiple credit lines invokes a similar art. Each line of credit represents a distinctive fragment, and it's careful synchronization that leads to the optimal outcome - a resplendent credit score. Let's delve into some expert tips to master this fine craft.

Unearthing the Power of Diversity

In the theater of credit management, diversity plays the protagonist. Tenacious credit champions recognize that a varied credit portfolio sends a message to creditors about their robust financial management skills. Managing a healthy mix of installment and revolving loans is perceived positively by lenders and contributes to your credit score.

Let's meet Emma, an aspiring homeowner. She juggles an auto loan, a couple of credit cards, and a university loan. Emma's diverse portfolio reflects her ability to manage various types of credit responsibly. Her potential mortgage lender will see this as evidence of Emma's discipline and dependability, positioning her favorably for loan approval.

Revising Balances: Know Your Ratios

One of the most critical numbers in your delicate dance with credit lines is your credit utilization ratio. This ratio, typically aiming for not more than 30%, demonstrates prudence and adherence to financial boundaries.

Consider the case of Jay, a young professional. Jay holds several credit cards and revels in the freedom they offer. Over time, however, Jay's usage creeps up unchecked, and his credit utilization ratio teeters towards 60%. This triggers alarm bells at the credit bureaus, resulting in a dip in Jay's credit score.

To avoid falling into the same trap as Jay, conduct regular audits of your credit usage. Ensure you maintain an overall healthy credit utilization ratio, and aim for efficient distribution across your different lines of credit.

Payment Discipline: Never Miss a Beat

Each line of credit sings its tune in the credit symphony, and maintaining payment discipline is akin to keeping beat with the music. Each missed or late payment introduces a discordant note, disrupting the harmony and pulling your credit score downwards.

Successful credit champions prioritize their payments and have a system in place to avoid missing due dates. Be it setting reminders, automating payments, or allocating funds as per due dates in their budget - every strategy is designed to ensure timely payments, maintaining the symphony of their credit score.

The Magic of Aging: Let Time Work its Charm

Patience adds maturity to wines and wisdom to minds. Credit lines are no different, with age adding to their charm. Older accounts bolster your credit age, enhancing your credit score.

Ella has been meticulously using a credit card for ten years. This ageing marvel of her credit portfolio significantly aids her credit score, demonstrating stability and long-term financial commitment.

Avoid prematurely closing out old credit accounts, especially without a valid reason. Instead, let these aged credit accounts work their magic on your credit score over time.

The Grand Symphony: Coordinated Use of Your Credit Lines

Sophisticated credit users don't view their credit lines in isolation; they perceive them as part of an integrated whole. They recognize the need for a grand symphony of coordinated credit use.

Imagine you're conducting an orchestra where each line of credit represents a unique instrument. As a seasoned conductor, your task is to harmonize the music from each section to create an awe-inspiring symphony. Your secured and unsecured loans, credit cards, mortgages, and other lines of credit all contribute to the harmony of a stellar credit score.

Building a shining credit score while managing multiple lines of credit is undeniably a labor of careful strategy, discipline, and perseverance. However, the rewards (lower interest rates, easier loan approvals, and overall improved financial health) serve as motivation for maintaining this delicate dance.

14.4 Up-to-date on Policies: Stay Ahead
Navigating the Constant Change in Credit Landscape

In the ever-evolving world of finance, credit policies, rules, and regulations face continual updates and revisions. Thus, staying current on industry changes and compliance requirements is crucial not only for financial institutions but also for individuals managing their credit. Practical adaptability and informed strategic decisions hinge on understanding these alterations, and in turn, significantly impact credit health.

Building Awareness: Your Weapon Against Unfavorable Impact

As individuals burdened by low FICO scores seek methods to enhance their credit prospects and achieve financial stability, it becomes every bit as important to sustain these efforts over time. It is what transforms short-term gains into long-lasting financial freedom. Ergo, developing the habit of staying informed about policy changes is the key to longevity in financial success.

For someone committed to possessing a healthy credit score, being in tune with regulations and understanding how they affect personal finance is valuable.

Policies and legal frameworks related to the credit industry are subject to constant modifications. Implementing measures like the Credit CARD Act of 2009 or changes in reporting requirements for credit bureaus under the National Consumer Assistance Plan – these changes often directly affect individuals' credit scores and financial health.

Gaining awareness about policy changes helps identify potential repercussions, both positive and negative, and chart a well-informed course of action. Furthermore, staying informed helps address any misinformation or news that triggers financial panic.

The Source Code: Following Reliable Channels for Policy Updates

Navigating the vast ocean of financial updates and news requires a savvy compass. To remain current on credit policies and regulations, explore various reliable sources for information:

- **Government websites:** Official government websites provide authentic and accurate information on regulatory changes. Websites like the Consumer Financial Protection Bureau (CFPB) and the Federal Trade Commission (FTC) impart valuable resources.
- **Financial publications:** Reputable publications such as The Wall Street Journal, The Financial Times, or Forbes frequently cover policy changes and offer expert opinions and analyses.
- **Industry experts and influencers:** By following financial experts, influencers, and organizations on social media, you gain access to insights and interpretations of policy changes as they happen.

- **Education programs and webinars:** Finance-focused education programs, seminars, and webinars are opportunities for increasing understanding of policy updates and potential implications on your financial situation.

By staying informed through these reliable channels, you arm yourself with actionable knowledge that can be leveraged to your benefit.

- **Adapt and Flourish:** Implementing Changes to Your Credit Strategy
  Armed with valuable insights into policy changes, it is essential to integrate them into your credit management strategies. A swift and well-informed approach to the shifting credit landscape will serve to strengthen your financial health:
- **Revision of strategies**: As regulations evolve, it may necessitate alterations to strategies for managing credit scores. Re-examine your existing methods and update your approach accordingly.
- **Be proactive:** Taking a proactive stance in response to policy changes not only mitigates negative impacts but often presents new opportunities for improving credit health.
- **Seek professional advice:** When faced with complex policy updates or unprecedented financial challenges, consider consulting a financial advisor for professional and tailored guidance.

A real-life example of policy adaptation could involve learning that the tax deductions you once enjoyed for student loan interest have been repealed. By promptly educating yourself on the implications and alternatives, such as refinancing, you can minimize any negative impact on your financial well-being.

Embrace Financial Agility: Your Key to Credit Success

Staying up-to-date with financial policies equips you with the agility to make informed decisions, adapt your strategies, maintain a healthy credit score, and achieve lasting financial freedom. Treat this pursuit of knowledge as an investment in your long-term success in navigating the 'credit universe'. As you develop the habit of constantly learning and adapting, your financial skills will evolve, and you will gain the ability to protect and improve your credit consistently.

In summary, remaining knowledgeable and up-to-date about credit policies enables you to make informed decisions essential for maintaining a healthy credit score and achieving long-term financial freedom. Tracking reliable sources and engaging with educational opportunities will significantly improve your ability to navigate the ever-evolving financial landscape.

Chapter 15:
Your Financial Destiny Awaits: Embrace an 800+ FICO Score, and Beyond

15.1 The Journey to 800 and Beyond

The arduous trek towards a FICO score of 800 and beyond marks a transformative milestone in the pursuit of financial stability, security, and autonomy. Symbolizing the epitome of creditworthiness and trustworthiness, FICO scores in the 800-range unlock doors previously closed to those burdened by lower credit ratings. In this chapter, we shall delve into the crucial steps and strategies for achieving and maintaining such an exceptional credit score, enabling our readers to shape their financial destinies and embark on a journey filled with newfound opportunities and promises of economic freedom.

The Power of 800: Unshackling the Chains of Limited Credit

Credit scores of 800 and beyond bring forth a myriad of advantages, allowing individuals to capitalize on unparalleled borrowing opportunities and financial rewards. With an extraordinary credit score, a borrower gains access to preferential interest rates, higher loan approval rates, and superior credit card offers complete with low annual percentage rates (APRs), lucrative rewards, and plush perks.

An 800+ FICO score bestows opportunities to build wealth, accumulate assets, and expand one's financial horizons. As a beacon of unwavering trust, a high credit rating cements credibility with lenders and ushers in a world of limitless possibilities.

Laying the Groundwork: Constructing a Strong Credit Foundation

Embarking on a journey towards a sky-scraping credit score of 800 and beyond necessitates deliberate and calculated actions. Establishing a rock-solid foundation of sound credit habits forms the cornerstone of a triumphant credit journey. The following guidelines will propel you further along the path towards credit mastery:

Payment Punctuality: Consistently making payments on time accounts for a significant portion of every credit score. Maintaining an unblemished track record of prompt payments demonstrates reliability and boosts overall creditworthiness.

Credit Utilization Mastery: Keeping credit utilization rates below 30% exemplifies proficient control over debt, thereby contributing to a higher FICO score. Continuously monitoring and managing credit card balances for optimal utilization is critical.

Credit History Preservation: The age of credit history plays a considerable role in determining the FICO score. Therefore, refrain from closing long-standing accounts and employ a mix of long-term and short-term credit to strengthen your credit history.

Healthy Credit Diversity: Utilizing a diverse array of credit types, such as mortgages, auto loans, and personal loans – in addition to credit cards – reflects adept handling of multiple financial responsibilities and reinforces credibility.

Journeying Towards the 800 FICO Summit: Overcoming Obstacles and Pitfalls
The ascent to an 800+ FICO score can be fraught with challenges and setbacks. Remaining vigilant against pitfalls that hamper credit health is pivotal:

Defending Against Fraud: Safeguarding one's credit against identity theft and fraud must remain a priority. Regularly monitor credit reports, use strong passwords, and enroll in monitoring services to thwart potential threats.

Steering Clear of High-Interest Debt: Keeping high-interest debt, such as payday loans or cash advances, at bay helps preserve financial stability. Opt for other borrowing options featuring lower interest rates instead.

Avoiding Late Payments and Collections: Late payments can severely dent credit scores. Automate payments, set reminders, and communicate with lenders about impending financial difficulties to circumvent negative impacts on your credit journey.

Navigating the 800 FICO Landscape: Unlocking Rewards and Opportunities
Upon reaching the coveted 800+ FICO score, bask in an array of benefits and privileges:

Negotiating Lower Interest Rates: Armed with exceptional creditworthiness, renegotiate lower interest rates on existing loans and credit cards, reducing debt and financial strain.

Bolstering Financial Reserves: Seize high credit score advantages to build an emergency fund, invest intelligently, and maintain loan approval cushions for unexpected financial needs.

Elevating Lifestyle and Well-being: Capitalize on luxury credit cards, prime memberships, and elite loyalty programs to indulge in unparalleled experiences, savings, and comfort.

Achieving a FICO score of 800 and beyond symbolizes mastery over one's financial life, creating a canvas of seemingly boundless economic possibilities. However, maintaining and nurturing this exclusive credit rating mandates unwavering commitment to personal financial growth, strategic planning, and resolute adaptability. It is a journey that challenges conventional wisdom and requires a deep dive into the intricacies of credit. Ultimately, the ubiquitous pursuit of a magnificent FICO score paves the way to real financial freedom, a life unencumbered by the constraints of cumbersome debt, and the blossoming of dreams initially deemed implausible.

15.2 Enjoying the Perks of High Credit Scores

Securing a high FICO score of 800 and beyond is quite similar to scaling the highest peak of a mountain - it requires perseverance, strategic planning, and diligence. Once at the pinnacle, the panoramic view of opportunities and benefits is breathtaking, characterized by preferential interest rates, premium credit card offers, easy loan approvals, and the ultimate luxury of financial stability.

To fully comprehend the windfall of privileges that an optimum FICO score offers, let us take a walk through the wealth-filled and limitless landscape of an 800+ credit score, abounding in unmatched perks and notable advantages.

An Oasis of Convenient Borrowing Opportunities

When your FICO score crosses the 800-mark, you become a darling among lenders. Banks, credit card issuers, and mortgage companies are eager to extend you credit in the form of prime loans, premium credit cards, and mortgage offers. This is because an elite credit score is seen as an assurance that the borrower will adhere to repayment schedules, reducing lending risk.

Let's imagine Sarah, a hardworking mother of three, looking to buy a new home. Her credit score, currently above 800, opens the floodgates to superior home mortgage deals, offering the lowest interest rates and flexible terms. She faces minimal hurdles in her home-buying journey and can, thus, focus her energies on finding the perfect home for her family. Sarah's story is an example of how a high credit score smooths out the wrinkles on the path of major life decisions.

An Array of Impressive Credit Card Perks

Owning an exceptional credit score means being on the wish list of premium credit card issuers. Companies like American Express, Chase, and Discover are willing to go out of their way to attract high-score holders with irresistible offers. The galaxy of perks can include generous cash-back programs, robust points systems, airline miles, hotel benefits, priority customer service, and even exclusive access to events and concerts.

Picture John, a twenty-something programmer, an ardent traveler, and an admirer of luxury. His 800+ credit score does not just ensure high credit card approval rates, but also an opportunity to choose from cards boasting top-flight benefits, from complimentary travel insurance to access to airport lounges worldwide. These perks make John's wanderlust more affordable and his journey pleasant and memorable.

The Comfort of Financial Readiness

Statistically, individuals with a high FICO score are typically better prepared for financial emergencies. They can secure lines of credit or loans at short notice due to their creditworthiness, enabling them to weather an unexpected storm without needing to deplete their savings or resort to high-interest short-term loans.

Consider Paula, a single parent with a high 800+ credit score. In an unfortunate circumstance where her car breaks down, she can swiftly take a low-interest loan or use her credit card to cover the cost of the repair. Her high credit score allows her to manage this surprise expenditure without causing significant financial stress and while preserving her savings for her child's future needs.

Achieving Your Aspiration for Financial Autonomy and Prosperity

The tangible perks of a high credit score, such as low borrowing costs and luxurious card benefits, are undoubtedly alluring. However, the real jewels in the crown are the intangible shield of financial security, the gift of autonomy, and the fulfillment of attaining economic success, each lending a sense of control and contentment.

For Jake, a self-employed entrepreneur with a coveted 800+ score, this control means having the power to expand his business when he sees fit without worrying about prohibitive interest rates. For Alice, climbing out of the poor credit rut into the 800+ zone granted her the confidence that she's on the right path towards financial stability, paving the way for an anxiety-free, restful night of sleep.

Enjoying the lavish benefits of a high FICO score is not merely about leveraging financial instruments to benefit from reduced rates or accruing travel miles. It's about adopting a changed perspective towards financial self-sufficiency and success, leading to an enriched life away from money-related stress, providing peace of mind and the capacity to focus on one's personal milestones rather than the next installment payment.

15.3 Continual Growth: Next-level Credit Master Strategies

our journey to credit mastery does not end once you have achieved an impressive 800+ FICO score; it is, in fact, only the beginning of an ongoing pursuit of excellence that paves the way for immense financial freedom and security. Continuous growth and improvement require implementing an array of next-level credit master strategies that are essential to maintaining your impressive credit history and staying ahead of the curve.

Creating a Strong Foundation: Diversify Your Credit Portfolio

Diversification is a crucial aspect of maintaining a high credit rating, as it demonstrates your ability to responsibly manage an assortment of credit types. Expanding your credit portfolio strategically includes a mix of installment loans, such as mortgages or auto loans, and revolving credit products like credit cards and lines of credit. Prudent diversification will not only help you achieve a robust credit profile but also protect your FICO score against fluctuations caused by unexpected financial events and market changes.

Staying Ahead: Keep Your Credit Utilization Low

While you may have already mastered the art of responsible credit card usage, it is vital to consistently maintain low credit utilization to preserve your outstanding FICO score. Credit utilization refers to the percentage of your available credit that is being used; experts recommend keeping it below 30% across all credit cards. By regularly monitoring your utilization rate and adjusting your spending habits accordingly, you will reassure lenders of your responsible use of credit, thereby safeguarding your high credit rating.

Building Lasting Relationships: Cultivating Long-Standing Accounts

Many individuals are unaware of the fact that the average age of their credit accounts has a significant impact on their overall FICO score. Having older, well-maintained accounts is viewed positively by credit bureaus, as it provides a more extensive history of your credit management abilities. Remember to periodically use your oldest cards, regardless of their attached benefits, in order to retain these accounts and contribute to creating a lasting history that signals your creditworthiness.

Strengthening Your Circle of Trust: The Power of Authorized Users
A powerful strategy to improve the overall average age of your credit accounts is to leverage the technique of becoming an authorized user on someone else's credit card. By joining in as an authorized user on a family member or close friend's credit card account with a long credit history and high credit limit, you can effectively incorporate their positive payment history into your own credit report. Ensure your trusted relationship remains untouched by discussing the terms of usage, repayment, and other responsibilities before becoming an authorized user.

Stay Proactive: Monitor Your Credit and Identify Fraudulent Activity
Vigilance is the key to maintaining your hard-earned credit score. By regularly reviewing your credit reports, you can spot any inconsistencies or errors that may negatively impact your credit. Set up a routine to request your free annual reports from all three major credit bureaus: Experian, TransUnion, and Equifax. In addition, investing in identity theft protection and credit monitoring services can provide added security and alerts in case of any suspicious activities or unauthorized changes.

Continuous Improvement: Adapt to New Credit Models and Legislation
The dynamic world of credit scoring and reporting is a constantly changing landscape that warrants continuous monitoring and education. Remain informed about evolving credit models, such as VantageScore and FICO's newer versions, which may introduce adjustments affecting your credit rating. Additionally, keep up-to-date with changes in credit and lending legislations that can potentially impact your rights, options, and borrowing costs. By staying informed and adapting your strategies, you ensure lasting credit mastery and success.

Through the application of these advanced credit master strategies, you can maintain and enhance your credit prowess, which will provide long-term financial stability and an ongoing sense of control and confidence. In this world of constant innovation and economic fluctuations, one must stay ever-vigilant and proactive in order to protect their creditworthiness and achieve financial freedom. By never settling for mediocrity and always striving for improvement, you will undoubtedly secure your place among the ranks of the true credit masters.

15.4 Credit Mastery: Your Key to Financial Freedom

Unveiling the treasure chest of financial freedom starts with unlocking the wisdom of credit mastery — transforming credit from being a source of stress to becoming a force of empowerment. This continuous journey requires commitment, dedication, and perseverance. But reach its end, and you will thrash away the shackles of limited opportunities and high-interest rates. With your FICO score standing strong and steady above 800, you will be driving along the highway to financial freedom and prosperity.

Cultivating a Credit Mindset

The first step towards achieving credit mastery involves adopting a credit mindset. It isn't about merely understanding lines of credit or maintaining a good score. It's about imbibing the essence of credit into every financial decision you make, with an eye always on your credit health.

Consider the journey of Amanda, a 42-year-old single mother of two. Amanda began her journey towards financial freedom with a credit score of 550, burdened by high debt and negative entries in her credit report. Working two jobs and raising her children, she couldn't afford the high interest rates on her debts.

Amanda started her journey by transforming her financial troubles into opportunities for growth. Instead of seeing credit as a burden, she perceived it as a tool - a way to unlock opportunities and increase her financial independence.
She focused on curating her resources, limiting her expenses, and consistently paying off her debts. This isn't only about financial strategy, but a profound attitudinal shift towards credit - an understanding that her choices now had longer-term implications for her financial health.

Over time, her score steadily grew, reflecting her changing mindset. And a day arrived when she not only crossed the 800 mark but also bought a house under her name for her children. Amanda's credit mindset freed her from the burdens of a poor credit score and gave her financial stability previously unknown.

Nurturing Long-term Financial Resilience

Credit mastery isn't a destination; it's a journey of cultivating financial resilience for the long haul. It's about a sustained commitment to responsible credit behaviors, even when they are tough and demand patience.

Let's take James as an example. A tech entrepreneur, James had long-since mastered his credit score. However, after a risky business investment, he found himself grappling with financial challenges. His FICO score didn't collapse overnight, but he saw where he was headed.

Armed with his credit mastery, James did not let adversity overpower him. He realigned his priorities, paid off as much debt as possible, even at the expense of his lifestyle. This robust response reflected his commitment to nurturing his credit score, even in the face of hardship. Due to his sustained efforts and credit-oriented mindset, he was able to maintain his high FICO score and stave off financial disaster.

Living the Perks of a High FICO Score

The throbbing heart of financial freedom lies in living the perks of a healthy credit score. High creditworthiness can transform your life, enabling access to loans with conducive terms and low interest rates, substantial savings on insurance premiums, and better opportunities for job applications and rentals.

George, a young professional, uses his 820 FICO score to live a life revolved around low-interest rates, high credit limits, and financial stability. From obtaining advantageous rates on mortgage and auto loans to using his credit card to reap rewards, George's high FICO score brings him moments of joy through his attractive financial opportunities.

Mastery over credit is a ceaseless journey towards financial well-being and prosperity. With an impenetrable shield of 800+ FICO score, you aren't just surviving; you are thriving in the ever-complex universe of personal finance. Your financial destiny indeed waits beyond credit mastery: A world glowing in the warm light of financial freedom and tranquility.

Conclusion

As you reach the closing pages of Credit Secrets: 2024 Edition - Leverage New, Powerful Insider Tactics & Proven 609 Letter Templates to Master an 800+ FICO Score. Your Path to Boundless Financial Freedom & Unmatched Security, you should feel proud of the journey you have embarked on. This book has provided you with an arsenal of groundbreaking strategies, insightful guidance, and proven methods to achieve credit mastery. We trust that with diligence, determination, and the practical wisdom gleaned from these pages, you are now poised to unlock a future of unlimited financial possibilities.

No longer should you feel held back by a low credit score, entangled in predatory lending webs, or daunted by the challenges of rebuilding your credit. By embracing the empowering insights put forth in this book, tailored to meet the needs of real people with real financial goals, you have taken charge of your financial life. You have set a course to rise like the phoenix, transforming your credit score into a symbol of resilience and strength, boldly navigating the ever-evolving landscape of credit, and charting a path to a gleaming horizon of burgeoning prosperity.

As you continue on this journey, remember that credit mastery is not a sprint; it's a marathon. Like all aspects of life, mastering your financial health requires continuous learning, adaptation, and perseverance. This book is only the beginning—a stepping stone towards your ultimate destination of boundless financial freedom and unmatched security.

But, never forget—you are not alone. These words on the pages shall remain your steadfast companions as you forge ahead, gently reminding you that the secrets to credit success lie within your grasp, your determination, and the way you wield the wisdom garnered from this illuminating tome. Revisit these pages often, celebrate your triumphs, and reflect on your setbacks, for each will be a lesson worth cherishing.

As you forge a new chapter in your life, now equipped with the knowledge and tools necessary to attain your financial objectives, we hope that the moment comes when you stand tall, basking in the glow of your elevated 800+ FICO score. May your future be filled with boundless opportunities, flourishing endeavors, and the unmatched security that only comes from being a credit champion.

Here's to a life unshackled, to dreams realized, to tides turned, and to walking the path illuminated by the beacon of financial freedom.

Thank you for joining us on this transformative journey. May the credit force be with you, now and always.

11
WORD
PHRASE

Table of Content

Chapter 1
Introduction: The 11 Magic Words to Boost Your Credit

1.1 Brief explanation of the potential of these words to improve credit.

Imagine having a set of words that can shift the power dynamic between you and credit agencies, that can make your requests not only heard but considered seriously. The **11 Magic Words** are carefully chosen expressions, each carrying a distinct impact designed to address credit challenges, improve credit profiles, and strengthen one's financial position. In this chapter, we'll uncover the potential of these words, demonstrating how simple language can become a potent tool for achieving concrete financial changes. These words aren't merely about enhancing vocabulary; they're strategic elements, empowering readers to actively improve their credit and financial security.

Words hold incredible power, especially when directed towards financial institutions, where every communication can influence your financial standing. Each word in this set is tailored to unlock specific outcomes, whether it's clarifying a credit discrepancy, negotiating better terms, or building a credible credit history. Unlike routine credit management advice, these words aren't about passive measures but are actionable tools that you can use in letters, emails, or phone conversations with creditors and agencies. Their purpose is to create clear, effective exchanges that credit representatives and agencies are more likely to respond to favorably.

Why Language Matters in Credit Interactions

The impact of language on credit is rooted in how credit agencies operate. These institutions manage vast volumes of information daily, including countless communications from consumers. Messages that are concise, clear, and authoritative command attention, especially when they follow a structured approach. Using the 11 Magic Words is about mastering this structured approach. When you communicate with clarity and authority, creditors and agencies see you as an informed individual—someone who understands the credit system and whose requests are worth considering seriously. This perception is key, as agencies are more inclined to act on behalf of individuals who appear knowledgeable and precise.

In an industry where financial institutions adhere strictly to protocols, understanding the power of language is essential. These words are designed to align with that formality, striking a balance between assertiveness and professionalism. For example, instead of a vague request for correction, a phrase built on the 11 Magic Words might read, "Please verify and correct the stated inaccuracy based on evidence provided." Such a statement is assertive, but more importantly, it's specific and actionable. Credit agents, trained to prioritize clear, actionable messages, are more likely to respond positively to such structured language.

Shaping Perceptions with the 11 Magic Words

The way creditors perceive your communication can influence their willingness to assist you. The 11 Magic Words are crafted to establish a credible, solution-oriented stance. For example, instead of using language that may come across as confrontational or unclear, these words guide you towards statements that are firm yet respectful. This approach positions you not as a passive account holder but as an informed party actively involved in shaping your financial profile. This shift in perception can lead to more favorable outcomes, from quicker response times to more lenient terms and conditions.

Moreover, credit agencies often value transparency, and these words help convey that. Using phrases rooted in transparency and accountability signals to creditors that you are open and truthful. This is particularly useful if you're disputing a charge or requesting a correction. Credit agents can respond more positively when they feel they're working with someone who values clarity and integrity, attributes that the 11 Magic Words subtly convey through phrases designed for transparency and respect.

Building Confidence in Credit Management

Beyond simply enhancing interactions, these words are also about building personal confidence. Credit improvement often feels daunting, especially when you're faced with complex reports, unfamiliar terminology, and rigid processes. By providing a specific vocabulary tailored for credit improvement, the 11 Magic Words offer a sense of control over the process. With each successful communication, whether it's a dispute letter or a payment negotiation, you'll feel more empowered and capable of navigating the credit landscape with authority.

This confidence isn't merely psychological. It has practical implications, as feeling in control makes you more likely to follow through with your credit management plans consistently. For instance, once you see the impact of the phrase "please provide detailed documentation," you're more likely to engage proactively with credit agencies, knowing that your words have the potential to elicit meaningful responses. This empowerment transforms credit improvement from a reactive to a proactive process, where you take steps toward specific goals with assurance.

Increasing the Likelihood of Positive Outcomes

Credit agencies and creditors respond best to messages that are purposeful, polite, and precise. The 11 Magic Words facilitate this by turning requests into direct, actionable items. A statement like, "Please verify this transaction and provide supporting documentation" is more effective than vague expressions of dissatisfaction. It shows that you're clear on what you need and know how to ask for it. In credit management, specificity increases the chances of receiving positive responses. The 11 Magic Words are engineered for this purpose, creating a consistent, professional impression across all interactions.

To further illustrate, if a consumer has been mistakenly charged and wants to request a reversal, a phrase like, "I request immediate correction of this error in accordance with FCRA guidelines" is far more effective than simply stating, "Please fix this." The specificity not only directs the agent towards a solution but also signals that you understand your rights and expect them to be upheld. These phrases are your tools for engaging in effective, legally grounded communication that aligns with the language creditors are trained to respect and respond to.

Setting a Foundation for Future Interactions

The 11 Magic Words aren't just single-use tools; they set a tone for ongoing communication. Once you establish yourself as someone who communicates clearly and purposefully, this reputation follows you through future interactions. Credit agents and agencies keep records of previous communications, so building a history of effective, respectful language can make each successive request more impactful. Over time, this positions you as a credible, reliable communicator, which is invaluable in maintaining a positive credit profile.

In short, the potential of the 11 Magic Words goes beyond immediate results. These words are building blocks for a reputation as a competent and credible individual in the eyes of credit agencies and creditors. With each interaction, you lay the foundation for a stronger, more resilient credit profile, where your words and actions consistently align, opening doors to new financial opportunities.

1.2 Purpose of This Section: Helping You Use Language to Achieve Concrete Results

The purpose of this section is clear: to show you how to use language strategically to get results that directly impact your credit profile. While most guides to improving credit offer general advice on debt management, payment history, or dispute tactics, this section is different. Here, we're focusing on the language itself as a tool. Every phrase, every word you choose to communicate with creditors, collection agencies, or credit bureaus plays a role in determining how they respond to you. By using the 11 Magic Words purposefully, you can steer conversations and requests toward the outcomes you need.

Language is often overlooked in financial contexts, but its impact is undeniable. Credit agencies and financial institutions rely on specific protocols when responding to requests, disputes, or negotiations. Knowing how to phrase these interactions with precision is key to capturing their attention. The goal isn't just to ask for what you want—it's to ask for it in a way that increases the chances of success. Every phrase should be designed to cut through bureaucratic noise, convey credibility, and direct the recipient toward actionable solutions that work in your favor.

Using Language as a Tactical Advantage

When you approach credit improvement as a tactical endeavor, you realize that language isn't just a passive medium but an active force. Each interaction you have with creditors or agencies becomes a strategic opportunity to influence how they perceive and prioritize your request. The 11 Magic Words aren't just arbitrary terms; they are chosen to make your communications sound authoritative, intentional, and difficult to ignore. The purpose here is to give you practical tools so that each message you send does more than just inform—it initiates change.

Think of these words as levers in a negotiation. They don't demand or plead but rather set the stage for clear and favorable resolutions. They serve as prompts that guide the reader toward specific actions, whether it's correcting a mistake, adjusting a credit entry, or clarifying account details. By approaching credit management in this way, you're not just communicating—you're directing the narrative and influencing outcomes.

Shifting From Reactive to Proactive Credit Management

Most people approach credit improvement reactively, responding to problems as they arise. The purpose of this section is to help you shift from a reactive mindset to a proactive one. Instead of waiting for a problem to show up in your credit report, these words allow you to take charge of each interaction. By using the 11 Magic Words in various contexts, you're positioning yourself as an informed and proactive individual, one who understands not just the importance of good credit but how to maintain and enhance it through intentional communication.

For instance, using phrases like "please verify" or "provide supporting documentation" in the correct context signals to creditors that you understand your rights and expect transparency. Rather than waiting for them to lead the conversation, you're setting a standard for how the interaction should proceed. This proactive approach not only builds your confidence but also compels agencies to take you more seriously, potentially leading to faster and more favorable responses.

Fostering Trust and Accountability in Communications

Trust and accountability are essential in any interaction with financial institutions, and your language is one of the best ways to establish both. By using the 11 Magic Words thoughtfully, you can convey a sense of integrity and professionalism that earns respect from creditors and agencies alike. The purpose of this section, therefore, is not only to teach you what words to use but also to help you create a style of communication that fosters trust and accountability on both sides.

When you frame your requests using precise language, you're showing that you're both informed and respectful of the process. This approach tends to yield better results than vague or emotionally charged language, which can sometimes put the recipient on the defensive. Instead, the 11 Magic Words enable you to build a reputation as someone who values fair dealings, is clear about their expectations, and knows how to work within the framework of credit protocols.

Achieving Specific Results, One Interaction at a Time

This section is designed to help you achieve measurable results with every interaction you initiate. Whether you're working to remove an error from your report, request a goodwill adjustment, or negotiate better terms, the language you use will play a decisive role in the outcome. Each time you communicate with a creditor or agency using these words, you're one step closer to your credit improvement goals. The purpose here is to provide you with repeatable, practical language strategies that allow you to tackle each situation with confidence.

For example, if you're disputing an inaccurate charge, a phrase like, "I request immediate verification of this transaction" is more than a polite query—it's a directive that leaves little room for ambiguity. It requires the credit bureau to act in a specific way, ensuring that your request is not only understood but prioritized. Over time, as you apply these phrases to various scenarios, you'll start to see a pattern of positive results, demonstrating the real-world effectiveness of strategic language in credit management.

Equipping You for Continuous Progress

Finally, the purpose of this section is to equip you with a skill set that extends beyond one-time fixes. Language is a powerful, flexible tool, and learning to use it effectively is a skill that grows with practice. With each successful application of the 11 Magic Words, you're building a foundation for continuous progress. This isn't just about improving your credit score in the short term but about mastering a communication style that will benefit you in every financial interaction moving forward.

Ultimately, this section is about empowerment. By giving you these words and showing you how to use them, the goal is to turn credit improvement into a manageable, achievable task. Each time you apply these phrases, you're reinforcing a pattern of success that builds on itself, leading to lasting, tangible improvements in your credit profile.

Chapter 2
The 11 Magic Words: Complete List and Meaning

2.1 The words with a brief explanation of why they work.

In this chapter, we dive into the heart of what makes these 11 words transformative tools for improving credit. Each word carries weight and purpose, designed to help you navigate financial communications with precision and authority. These words aren't selected at random; they're each tailored to address typical responses from creditors and credit agencies, making it possible to turn a simple request into an actionable, results-oriented conversation. By understanding why these words work and how to use them, you'll be able to approach each credit-related situation with the right language to drive favorable outcomes.

1. "Verify"

"Verify" is a powerful request that implies thoroughness. It asks for confirmation and evidence, which is particularly useful when disputing errors or clarifying charges on your credit report. When you ask a credit bureau or creditor to "verify" information, you're not just asking for a check—you're demanding proof. This word is vital for situations where a claim or entry might be inaccurate, pushing the agency to validate the information they've provided. It emphasizes accountability and transparency, critical in credit reporting.

2. "Correct"

The word "correct" is direct and actionable. When used in communication, it indicates that you've identified an issue and expect it to be resolved. Unlike words like "fix" or "adjust," which can sound vague, "correct" leaves no room for ambiguity. It's particularly effective in letters addressing discrepancies, such as errors on a credit report. When you request a correction, you're signaling that the issue is specific and requires a clear response.

3. "Document"

Asking for "documentation" transforms your request from casual to formal. Creditors and bureaus deal with a high volume of requests, but a demand for documentation elevates your inquiry, demonstrating that you expect an official, detailed response. By requesting "documentation," you're not only protecting your rights but also gathering evidence that could be crucial if further disputes or escalations are needed. This word encourages thoroughness, nudging agencies to take your inquiry seriously.

4. "Provide"

"Provide" is a respectful yet firm request that communicates expectation. When you ask a creditor or agency to "provide" specific information, it emphasizes the expectation of receiving a complete, clear answer. It's a term that can be used in any context where you're requesting something specific, such as an account history or a list of actions taken. The word "provide" gives you authority without being overly assertive, positioning your request as reasonable and clear.

5. "Dispute"

"Dispute" is a term with legal weight in the world of credit. When you state that you "dispute" an entry, it conveys that you believe it to be incorrect and are formally questioning its accuracy. This is a term that credit bureaus and creditors must respect under the Fair Credit Reporting Act, and it initiates a process that they are obligated to respond to. By using "dispute," you're invoking your rights and setting in motion a legally binding response.

6. "Review"

"Review" is a term that encourages a second look without assigning fault. It's useful for situations where you need an entry re-evaluated, like a late payment or a high balance. By requesting a "review," you're suggesting there may be an alternative perspective that wasn't previously considered, inviting the recipient to revisit the details without implying error. This word is particularly effective in situations where you're seeking leniency or understanding from a creditor.

7. "Confirm"

"Confirm" is a powerful way to solidify facts. When you ask for confirmation, you're expecting a concrete statement that either supports or denies a particular claim. For example, if you've negotiated a payment arrangement, asking the creditor to "confirm" the details in writing protects you by ensuring both parties agree on the terms. It's a word that implies finality, setting clear expectations and establishing a record of agreement.

8. "Request"

While it might seem simple, "request" has a polite authority. It's both courteous and firm, demonstrating that while you're asking for assistance or adjustment, you expect to be taken seriously. Using "request" in correspondence is especially valuable when dealing with goodwill adjustments or fee waivers. The word itself suggests that you're making a reasonable appeal, one that deserves careful consideration.

9. "Immediately"

"Immediately" is a word that conveys urgency. When you include this term in a request, you signal that prompt attention is needed. This word is especially effective for time-sensitive issues, such as preventing the reporting of a missed payment. However, it should be used sparingly to avoid coming across as demanding. "Immediately" is ideal for circumstances where you need rapid action to prevent or correct an issue that could affect your credit.

10. "Accurate"

The word "accurate" frames the conversation around correctness and precision. By emphasizing that you expect "accurate" information, you're holding the credit bureau or creditor to a high standard, pushing them to meet it. This term is particularly effective when addressing potential errors in credit reporting. Requesting accuracy is a professional way to demand quality, signaling that you value precision in all dealings affecting your credit.

11. "Reconsider"

"Reconsider" is a strategic term for negotiations or appeals. It's useful for situations where you've received an unfavorable response, such as a denied credit increase or refused fee waiver. Asking an institution to "reconsider" implies that circumstances may have changed or additional information is available, suggesting a second chance without directly challenging the first decision. This word invites a fresh review, which can sometimes open the door to a more favorable outcome.

Why These Words Matter

Each of these words has been selected not just for its meaning but for the psychological and procedural impact it has on the recipient. They are designed to work within the credit system's formal structure, speaking the language that credit bureaus, creditors, and agencies understand and respect. By incorporating these words into your communications, you are not just requesting a change—you are shaping how the request is perceived, processed, and acted upon.

These words work because they strike a balance between authority and respect. They are strong enough to demand attention but professional enough to maintain a positive tone, a crucial factor in any interaction with financial institutions. Credit bureaus and creditors are accustomed to dealing with requests daily, but requests framed with precision and professionalism often stand out, moving them to action more effectively than vague or confrontational language.

The goal here is to help you harness the power of language in a structured, purposeful way, making every interaction count toward your credit improvement. When used correctly, these words can elevate your communications, compelling creditors and agencies to see you as an informed, assertive individual whose requests warrant serious consideration.

2.2 How they can influence interactions with creditors and credit agencies.

The 11 Magic Words aren't just a collection of phrases—they're a strategic framework designed to influence how credit bureaus, creditors, and collection agencies perceive and respond to your communications. Each word has been selected for its ability to engage with the credit industry's processes, language, and expectations. When used correctly, these words have the power to shift an interaction from passive or dismissive to responsive and attentive, amplifying your authority in situations where precision is essential. By aligning with industry standards and expectations, these words create a tone of professionalism and command, compelling these institutions to respond with greater accountability and often leading to more favorable results.

Creating Authority and Credibility

When communicating with credit bureaus or creditors, authority and credibility are everything. Credit agents receive countless requests daily, often lacking specificity or clarity. The 11 Magic Words work to immediately differentiate your communication from the rest, positioning you as an informed and proactive individual who understands the credit system. Words like "verify," "provide," and "document" signal to the recipient that you aren't approaching this interaction casually. Instead, you are setting expectations and making it clear that you know your rights and are prepared to advocate for them effectively.

Credit agents and bureau representatives are trained to recognize and respond to clear, authoritative language. For example, if you're disputing an error on your credit report, stating, "Please verify this transaction with supporting documentation," establishes a tone that goes beyond a simple request. It conveys that you are seeking a substantiated response and expect thoroughness. This subtle but strategic language shifts the interaction from one where you are merely "asking" to one where you are "directing," encouraging the recipient to treat your request with the seriousness it warrants.

Establishing Clarity and Reducing Misinterpretation

Clarity is critical when dealing with credit matters, as vague or ambiguous language can lead to misunderstandings, delays, or outright dismissals. The 11 Magic Words help ensure that your requests are not only clear but are also framed in terms that creditors and bureaus can easily understand and act upon. Words like "accurate" and "confirm" are direct and specific, leaving little room for misinterpretation. These terms emphasize a commitment to accuracy and transparency, making it difficult for the recipient to overlook or ignore your request.

By removing ambiguity from your communications, these words reduce the likelihood of back-and-forth exchanges or incomplete responses, both of which can stall progress on your credit objectives. A phrase such as, "Please correct the inaccurate information on my report" is precise and leaves no doubt about your expectations. The specificity inherent in these words aligns with the procedural mindset of credit agencies, which are more likely to respond effectively to clearly articulated instructions.

Prompting Action and Accountability

Credit agencies and creditors operate in a structured environment where responses are often templated and procedural. The 11 Magic Words are designed to break through this standardization, pushing for a tailored response rather than a generic reply. Words like "immediately" and "reconsider" prompt urgency and direct accountability, signaling that you expect not only a response but a timely and personal one. When you state that an issue needs to be addressed "immediately," it conveys urgency and encourages the recipient to prioritize your request over others that may lack such clarity.

Moreover, by using words that imply accountability—such as "document" and "confirm"—you compel credit representatives to act in ways that are traceable and verifiable. When an agent is required to "document" a change or "confirm" an agreement, they are often obligated to record these actions, creating a paper trail that can be valuable for future reference. This accountability discourages superficial responses and pushes agents to engage with your request more thoroughly, as their response can be referenced if needed for escalation or follow-up.

Building a Consistent, Respectful Tone

While assertiveness is essential, respect is equally important, especially when dealing with agencies that hold significant influence over your financial profile. The 11 Magic Words enable you to strike a balance between authority and politeness, creating a tone that commands respect without being confrontational. Words like "request" and "provide" embody this balanced approach, projecting professionalism and reasonableness in your communication. When you say, "I request an accurate update to this record," it's a firm directive, but it's also courteous, demonstrating that you are serious but fair in your expectations.

This respectful tone is crucial, as overly aggressive language can put credit agents on the defensive, potentially resulting in less cooperation. The 11 Magic Words guide you to express your needs effectively without crossing into adversarial territory. Creditors and agencies are more inclined to assist individuals who communicate with respect and clarity, as it fosters a collaborative atmosphere, even when addressing issues or disputes.

Creating a Record of Professional Communication

Credit interactions are rarely one-time events. Establishing a pattern of clear, professional communication with credit bureaus and creditors can be invaluable, especially if your case requires future follow-up or escalations. The 11 Magic Words help you build a record of communication that reflects a consistent, credible approach. Each time you use phrases like "verify" or "confirm," you're creating a trail of professionalism that reinforces your commitment to accuracy and fairness. This can be advantageous if disputes need to be escalated, as your past communications will demonstrate that you approached each interaction thoughtfully and professionally.

A well-documented record of clear communication also serves as a reference for you, allowing you to track the progression of your requests and follow up with confidence. Should a creditor or bureau fail to respond appropriately, you'll have documented proof that outlines your efforts and their responses (or lack thereof), which can be crucial in disputes or appeals. This cumulative effect of using the 11 Magic Words isn't just about influencing individual interactions; it's about establishing a long-term record of accountability and respect.

Enhancing the Likelihood of Favorable Outcomes

Ultimately, the 11 Magic Words are designed to increase the likelihood of positive outcomes in your credit interactions. Credit agencies and creditors are more responsive to language that is structured, respectful, and direct. By using these words to frame your requests, you create interactions that credit representatives are not only equipped to handle but are also more inclined to act upon favorably. This influence extends beyond simple changes or corrections; it establishes a professional rapport that can impact future dealings with these institutions.

For example, if you've successfully navigated a credit dispute with a particular bureau using precise and professional language, future interactions may be met with greater receptivity, as you've built a foundation of mutual respect and understanding. The cumulative effect of using the 11 Magic Words can thus create an environment where creditors and agencies view you as a knowledgeable individual who values accuracy and accountability—traits that are respected across the credit industry.

In summary, these 11 Magic Words influence interactions with creditors and credit agencies by creating authority, ensuring clarity, prompting accountability, establishing a professional tone, building a strong record, and increasing the likelihood of favorable outcomes. When used effectively, they transform routine credit interactions into opportunities for positive change, allowing you to take control of your financial narrative with confidence and precision.

Chapter 3
How to Use the 11 Words in Key Situations

3.1 Practical examples of phrases for contacting creditors, negotiating debts, and enhancing your credit profile.

Effectively applying the 11 Magic Words in real-life scenarios requires a blend of precision, assertiveness, and a professional tone. Whether you're reaching out to creditors, negotiating outstanding debts, or seeking improvements to your credit profile, having pre-defined, structured phrases can significantly increase your chances of success. Each of the examples provided here is crafted to communicate your request clearly while using the 11 Magic Words strategically to encourage positive responses from creditors, credit bureaus, or collection agencies.

1. Contacting Creditors for Account Discrepancies

When dealing with account discrepancies—like incorrect charges, late payment markings, or other errors on your credit report—it's essential to request verification and correction with clarity and authority. Here's a practical example that incorporates key words from the 11 Magic Words list to ensure your message is both professional and effective.

Example:

> *"Dear [Creditor's Name],*
> *I am contacting you regarding an entry on my credit report that I believe to be inaccurate. I respectfully request that you verify the accuracy of this record and provide supporting documentation to confirm its validity. If an error is identified, please correct the entry to reflect the accurate details. Thank you for your prompt attention to this matter."*

In this example, terms like "verify," "provide," and "correct" signal specific actions. You're not merely pointing out an error—you're asking the creditor to substantiate the record, encouraging accountability. This language also makes it clear that if an error is found, you expect a correction, positioning you as someone who values transparency and accuracy.

2. Negotiating a Debt Settlement or Payment Plan

Debt negotiations are often delicate, as they involve finding a balance between firmness and willingness to work with the creditor. In such cases, words like "request," "confirm," and "reconsider" can be invaluable, as they show both respect and assertiveness. Here's an example of how to frame a request for a debt settlement in a way that promotes understanding and cooperation.

Example:

> "Dear [Creditor's Name],
>
> I am reaching out to discuss my current outstanding balance and to request a mutually agreeable solution. Given my financial circumstances, I kindly request that you reconsider the current terms and explore the possibility of a reduced settlement amount or an extended payment plan. Please confirm any arrangements in writing so that we can proceed with a resolution that satisfies both parties. Thank you for considering my request."

By using "request," "reconsider," and "confirm," this message demonstrates your willingness to work collaboratively without conceding your need for fair and achievable terms. You're acknowledging the debt while respectfully asking for flexibility, making it easier for the creditor to respond positively. Confirming the arrangement in writing also sets a standard for transparency and accountability in future communications.

3. Enhancing Your Credit Profile by Requesting Goodwill Adjustments

Goodwill adjustments are requests you make to creditors asking them to remove negative entries (such as a late payment) from your credit report as a gesture of goodwill, especially if you've been a reliable customer otherwise. This situation benefits from using phrases that are courteous yet precise, ensuring your request is framed as a reasonable favor rather than a demand.

Example:

> "Dear [Creditor's Name],
>
> I am writing to request a goodwill adjustment to my credit report. Due to [specific reason, e.g., unforeseen circumstances], I was unable to make a payment on time. Since then, I have worked diligently to keep my account in good standing and am committed to maintaining a positive relationship with

[Company Name]. I respectfully request that you reconsider the late payment entry on my account, as a gesture of goodwill, to reflect my overall commitment to responsible credit management. I appreciate your understanding and consideration."

In this example, "request," "goodwill," and "reconsider" are used to frame the request respectfully, appealing to the creditor's sense of fairness without implying blame or entitlement. You are making it clear that you value the relationship and that the adjustment would align with your ongoing efforts to manage credit responsibly. This approach is professional and considerate, making it more likely that the creditor will respond favorably.

4. Disputing an Incorrect Entry on Your Credit Report

When disputing incorrect entries, such as an erroneous debt or mistaken identity case, clear and direct language is crucial. The following example shows how to firmly, yet respectfully, ask for a re-evaluation of an entry on your report.

Example:

"Dear [Credit Bureau's Name],
I am disputing an entry on my credit report related to [specific account or error]. I request that you review this entry and provide supporting documentation that verifies its accuracy. I believe this record to be incorrect, and I am seeking an accurate reflection of my credit history. If the entry cannot be verified, please remove it from my report. I appreciate your prompt attention to this matter and look forward to receiving confirmation of the outcome."

This message employs "dispute," "request," "verify," and "accurate" to set a tone of professionalism and expectation. By requesting verification, you're not accusing the bureau of wrongdoing but asking for clarity and substantiation. By positioning yourself as an informed individual expecting accuracy, you're prompting the bureau to act with precision.

5. Requesting Documentation to Resolve a Credit Issue

Sometimes, the key to resolving a credit issue lies in obtaining specific documents or proof of past communications. When requesting documentation, clarity is essential. The following example demonstrates how to phrase this request effectively.

Example:

"Dear [Creditor's Name],

I am writing to request documentation related to my account history. Please provide copies of all relevant statements, payment records, and correspondence to assist in resolving a discrepancy I have identified. Your assistance in providing this documentation will help ensure that my records remain accurate. Thank you for your cooperation and prompt response."

This example makes use of "request," "provide," and "accurate" to establish a professional and specific tone. By asking for documentation, you're underscoring the importance of transparency and precision. The request is courteous but firm, showing that you're prepared to review the details carefully.

6. Confirming Details of a Payment Agreement

Once you've reached an agreement with a creditor, confirming the details in writing is essential to avoid future misunderstandings. Here's how you might frame a message to ensure the terms are documented accurately.

Example:

"Dear [Creditor's Name],

Following our recent conversation regarding my payment plan, I would like to confirm the agreed-upon terms. Please provide written confirmation of the payment schedule, including amounts and dates, as discussed. This documentation will help ensure clarity for both parties and facilitate a smooth repayment process. Thank you for your cooperation."

Here, "confirm," "provide," and "clarity" are used to communicate the need for documented assurance. This wording is particularly helpful for long-term arrangements, ensuring both parties have a mutual understanding that can be referenced if needed. This proactive approach not only solidifies the agreement but also demonstrates your commitment to following through responsibly.

Enhancing Your Communications with Precision and Professionalism

Each of these examples demonstrates how strategically chosen language can guide interactions toward specific, favorable outcomes. By structuring requests with the 11 Magic Words, you ensure your messages are clear, respectful, and purposeful, creating an environment where creditors and bureaus are more likely to respond positively. Using these phrases effectively allows you to build a credit profile that reflects accuracy, transparency, and responsibility, transforming what might otherwise be stressful interactions into opportunities for growth and improvement.

3.2 Tips on adjusting tone and language for different contexts (letters, emails, phone calls).

Effectively communicating with creditors or credit bureaus requires not only the right words but also the right tone. The form of communication—whether a formal letter, an email, or a phone call—can dramatically influence the outcome of your interactions. Understanding how to adjust your language and tone to suit each context can make your requests more persuasive and increase the likelihood of a positive response. This section provides practical insights into tailoring your approach to suit each medium, ensuring that your message is both impactful and professional.

Letters: Formality and Precision

A written letter remains one of the most powerful ways to communicate with creditors and credit bureaus, particularly for formal requests such as disputes, goodwill adjustments, or error corrections. Letters offer a level of formality that inherently signals respect and seriousness, which can be particularly effective when dealing with credit reporting agencies or addressing longstanding credit issues.

When crafting a letter, your tone should be polite but authoritative. Avoid overly casual language and focus on clarity. Start with a brief introduction, stating your reason for writing. Use phrases like "I respectfully request" or "I am seeking verification" to convey a professional, respectful tone while establishing the purpose of your communication. Words from the 11 Magic Words, such as "verify," "correct," and "documentation," are especially effective here, as they demand clear action in a way that feels structured and objective.

Letters also provide an opportunity to create a written record of your requests, which can be essential for follow-up or legal purposes. Ending a letter with "Thank you for your prompt attention to this matter" or "I look forward to your confirmation" reinforces both professionalism and your expectation of a timely response. Remember, a letter is a tangible piece of communication that will be kept on file, so ensure it reflects your commitment to clarity and professionalism.

Emails: Efficiency and Accessibility

Emails offer a more accessible and efficient way to communicate with creditors, especially for routine inquiries, follow-ups, or clarifications on previously discussed matters. Although emails are generally less formal than letters, they still require a professional tone and concise structure. Because email communication is often quicker and less structured, the tone here should strike a balance between formality and accessibility.

In an email, it's important to get to the point quickly. Begin with a brief introduction or reference to previous correspondence if applicable, such as "Following up on our last conversation regarding…" or "I am reaching out to request an update on…" Use direct, respectful language, and avoid overly detailed explanations that may dilute the purpose of your message. Terms like "provide," "review," and "confirm" from the 11 Magic Words work well in emails, as they establish clear requests that are easy for the recipient to address.

A crucial aspect of email communication is closing effectively. Since email is a faster medium, end with a call to action or a request for a specific timeline, such as "Please let me know by [date] if further information is needed" or "I look forward to receiving confirmation of this arrangement." These closing statements set expectations and encourage prompt responses, which can be beneficial if the matter requires timely attention.

Phone Calls: Personable and Collaborative

Phone calls, while less formal, provide an opportunity to establish rapport and make your case more personable. When you speak directly with a creditor or representative, you can use tone and pacing to convey your sincerity and professionalism. Phone calls are often best suited for initial inquiries, negotiations, or clarifying details about an agreement or entry on your report. The flexibility of a live conversation allows you to respond to questions or objections immediately, which can sometimes lead to quicker resolutions.

When speaking on the phone, use words like "verify," "confirm," and "request" strategically to keep the conversation focused and professional. For instance, you might say, "I'd like to confirm the terms we discussed" or "Could you verify the timeline for this correction?" These phrases keep the dialogue on track, signaling that you are informed and prepared to handle the matter at hand.

Another important aspect of phone communication is the tone of voice. Maintain a calm, polite, and professional demeanor, even if the representative is less than cooperative. Avoid sounding confrontational, as this can cause defensiveness. Instead, focus on collaboration by using phrases like, "I understand, but I'd like to clarify..." or "Could we explore another option?" This approach makes it clear that you are interested in finding a resolution that works for both parties, which is often received positively.

Ending a call effectively is crucial. Summarize any agreed-upon actions, repeating the details to ensure mutual understanding. For example, "Just to confirm, you'll be sending me the documentation by next week," or "I'll expect to hear back regarding the correction within [specific timeframe]." This reinforces accountability and provides you with verbal confirmation that can serve as a reference in future communications.

Adjusting Language for Context-Specific Needs

Each communication medium has its strengths, and knowing when to adapt your language for each is essential for effective credit management. A letter's formal tone is best suited for making structured, detailed requests that require documentation or serve as a long-term record. Emails, while less formal, offer efficiency for ongoing conversations and follow-ups. Phone calls, on the other hand, allow for immediate interaction, making them ideal for negotiations or clarifications.

By mastering the nuances of tone and language in each of these contexts, you create a consistent, professional image that strengthens your position in credit-related matters. Letters and emails emphasize written records and accountability, whereas phone calls emphasize personal connection and real-time responsiveness. When you adjust your language and approach to fit the medium, you not only enhance the clarity of your requests but also show creditors and bureaus that you're both knowledgeable and adaptable, qualities that command respect and encourage positive engagement.

Chapter 4
Strategies to Monitor Progress and Refine Your Approach

4.1 How to assess whether using the 11 words is delivering results.

When you set out to improve your credit by strategically applying the 11 Magic Words, assessing the effectiveness of this approach is crucial. Monitoring your progress not only ensures that your efforts are producing the intended results but also allows you to refine your approach based on real-world feedback. By establishing specific markers for success, tracking each communication, and reviewing changes to your credit profile, you can determine whether these 11 words are achieving their purpose. This section provides a structured approach to evaluating your progress, ensuring you can make informed adjustments to maximize the impact of your language.

Setting Clear Goals and Expectations

Before evaluating whether the 11 Magic Words are working, it's essential to set clear, measurable goals. Each time you send a letter, email, or make a phone call using these words, identify what you hope to achieve from that specific interaction. Are you looking to correct an error, secure a goodwill adjustment, or negotiate a lower interest rate? Define the desired outcome upfront and set a reasonable timeframe for response. Having a clear objective makes it easier to gauge whether the communication was successful and allows you to measure progress consistently.

For instance, if you send a request to "verify" a credit entry, your goal might be to receive documented confirmation or, if the entry is erroneous, to have it removed within 30 days. By setting this specific expectation, you have a defined basis to evaluate the success of your request. Document each goal and timeframe, as these records will provide an essential reference point for tracking your results.

Maintaining a Detailed Record of Communications

Effective progress assessment relies heavily on maintaining accurate records of every interaction. Keep a log of all communications, including the date, method (letter, email, or phone call), the purpose of the message, and the 11 Magic Words you used. Also, include any responses received, actions taken by the creditor or agency, and any follow-up actions you initiated. This log will become your evidence of progress, allowing you to see which strategies are yielding results and which may need refinement.

For each entry, note specific phrases used, such as "please provide documentation" or "request an immediate correction," along with the outcome. These records will help you determine patterns, identifying which words or phrases tend to be more effective in particular situations. Over time, this data-driven approach will allow you to refine your communications, focusing on the language that has proven most impactful in similar contexts.

Evaluating Response Quality and Timeliness

A key indicator of success is the quality and timeliness of responses from creditors or credit bureaus. Responses that are prompt, detailed, and address your request directly are positive indicators that the 11 Magic Words are having the desired impact. If you requested verification or correction and received a clear response within your expected timeframe, this signals that your communication was effective.

Conversely, if you receive vague or generic responses, or if creditors ignore your requests entirely, this could suggest that the chosen words did not carry the intended weight. In these cases, consider adjusting your language for future communications. Phrases like "please confirm receipt" or "provide supporting documentation" add clarity, signaling that you expect detailed responses. Analyze how often you receive prompt and comprehensive replies and use this information to fine-tune your approach.

Monitoring Credit Report Changes

Ultimately, the success of using the 11 Magic Words should be reflected in your credit report. Regularly monitoring your credit report is essential for understanding the impact of your efforts. Each time you initiate a request—whether for a correction, adjustment, or verification—check your credit report after a suitable period to see if the change has been implemented.

If you notice errors being corrected or old entries being removed, this is a tangible sign that your language is achieving results. Keep track of specific improvements, such as adjustments to your payment history, debt amounts, or the removal of outdated or inaccurate entries. Positive changes in your report directly indicate that the strategies you've applied with the 11 Magic Words are effectively enhancing your credit profile. However, if changes aren't reflected, this may be an opportunity to refine your approach, following up with an escalated request or modified language.

Adjusting Based on Patterns and Feedback

Part of assessing your progress involves recognizing patterns in responses and using this feedback to improve future communications. For instance, if certain creditors respond favorably to phrases like "please confirm" or "request documentation," make a note of this and apply similar phrasing in future interactions with the same or similar organizations. On the other hand, if specific requests go unanswered or result in unsatisfactory responses, consider adjusting your language, tone, or approach to increase the impact of your message.

Also, pay attention to feedback from creditors or credit bureaus, as it can provide insights into what they prioritize in communications. If a representative provides constructive feedback, such as suggesting specific documentation or noting that certain details are required, incorporate these elements in subsequent communications. This iterative approach allows you to refine your strategy continually, ensuring that each use of the 11 Magic Words becomes more effective based on past experiences.

Tracking Long-Term Impact on Credit Scores

While immediate improvements in your credit report can be encouraging, tracking the long-term impact on your credit score provides a more comprehensive measure of success. Over time, the cumulative effect of successful corrections, adjustments, and negotiations should be reflected in an improved credit score. Monitoring your score over months or even years provides an indication of how consistently effective your language strategies are, particularly if your score steadily improves as you apply the 11 Magic Words in various situations.

However, credit scores can fluctuate for multiple reasons, so consider tracking other aspects of your credit profile as well. Improved credit utilization rates, increased credit limits, and a cleaner payment history all contribute to a healthier credit score, and each can reflect the success of your communications. A steady upward trend in these areas validates that your approach is delivering sustainable results and that the 11 Magic Words are helping you create a positive, lasting impact on your financial health.

Reviewing and Refining for Continuous Improvement

Assessing whether the 11 Magic Words are delivering results is not a one-time task—it's an ongoing process that evolves as you interact with different creditors and encounter varying credit challenges. Set aside regular intervals, such as monthly or quarterly, to review your progress and identify areas for improvement. Look back on your communications log, analyze the response patterns, and evaluate changes in your credit report to see where adjustments might enhance your future effectiveness.

By regularly reviewing and refining your approach, you can ensure that the 11 Magic Words continue to deliver meaningful results. This continuous improvement strategy not only strengthens your credit profile but also empowers you with a deeper understanding of how language influences financial outcomes, positioning you for ongoing success in managing and enhancing your credit.

4.2 Guidelines to modify the strategy and maximize the impact of the magic words.

Using the 11 Magic Words effectively requires more than just memorizing a set of terms—it demands flexibility and awareness of how different scenarios evolve. Each interaction with creditors, credit bureaus, or collection agencies may call for nuanced adjustments in your approach. By refining your strategy and modifying your language to align with the context and response patterns, you can maximize the impact of these words. This section offers actionable guidelines on how to enhance your strategy, ensuring that your use of the Magic Words remains powerful, adaptive, and results-driven.

1. Tailor the Words to Fit the Specific Purpose

The effectiveness of the 11 Magic Words depends largely on how well they align with your specific objectives in each interaction. While each word is inherently impactful, applying them with precision to match your goals is crucial. For example, if your goal is to correct an error on your credit report, words like "verify" and "correct" should be central to your request. On the other hand, if you are negotiating a debt settlement, emphasizing words like "reconsider" or "confirm" may be more appropriate, as they prompt collaboration and accountability.

Adapting your choice of words based on context shows creditors and agencies that you are not merely sending generic requests but are thoughtfully addressing each situation with relevant language. This attention to detail makes it more likely that the recipient will respond in kind, treating your request with the seriousness it deserves.

2. Adjust Tone Based on Response History

Tracking response patterns allows you to make informed adjustments to your language and tone. For instance, if a creditor has been slow to respond or provides vague answers, it may be time to use more assertive language in your next communication. Phrases such as "immediate attention is required" or "confirm receipt of this request" can add a layer of urgency and prompt faster action.

Conversely, if a creditor or agency has been cooperative and responsive, using a collaborative tone that acknowledges their assistance can strengthen the relationship. Phrasing like, "Thank you for your previous assistance; I am reaching out to request an update" recognizes their past efforts, creating a sense of partnership. By adjusting your tone based on past interactions, you establish a rapport that can lead to more favorable outcomes in future communications.

3. Be Selective in Combining Words for Maximum Clarity

The 11 Magic Words are most effective when used strategically, not randomly. Overloading a single message with too many of these words can dilute the clarity of your request. Instead, focus on the two or three words that best capture the purpose of each interaction. For example, in a letter disputing an error, a combination like "verify," "document," and "accurate" conveys both your expectations and the level of detail you require.

Using a few carefully chosen words in each communication creates a clear, focused request that is easy for the recipient to act upon. Moreover, a well-structured request built around specific terms helps prevent misinterpretation, increasing the likelihood of a response that aligns with your needs.

4. Escalate Language When Initial Requests Are Ignored

If initial requests go unanswered or are met with unsatisfactory responses, it's time to escalate your language. Start by reinforcing the seriousness of your request with phrases like "I require confirmation" or "immediate verification is necessary." Escalation signals that you expect a response and are prepared to pursue further actions if necessary.

For ongoing issues, such as a repeated lack of response, you may need to use stronger language that implies potential escalation to regulatory bodies or dispute resolution services. For example, stating, "Failure to respond may require additional measures to ensure accuracy in my credit profile" implies that you are prepared to take further steps if your request is not addressed. This shift in language can prompt creditors to prioritize your request, recognizing that you are serious about seeing the matter resolved.

5. Reframe Requests to Reflect Changes in Strategy

If your initial approach does not yield the desired results, consider reframing your request using alternative Magic Words. For example, if a request for verification was denied or ignored, shifting to a request for "supporting documentation" might yield a different response. Sometimes, a slight rewording can be enough to clarify your expectations and prompt a more favorable outcome.

Reframing also applies to situations where you're negotiating. If initial terms are not accepted, try rephrasing your request using words that convey flexibility without compromising your core objectives. A phrase like, "I am open to reconsidering terms if supporting details are provided" shows a willingness to adapt while still maintaining your position. This adaptability often encourages creditors to respond constructively, knowing that you are both firm and fair.

6. Observe Response Timelines and Adapt Accordingly

The timing of responses from creditors and agencies can offer insights into the effectiveness of your strategy. Quick responses indicate that your language is resonating, while delays may signal that adjustments are needed. If responses are slower than expected, consider modifying your approach to emphasize urgency. For example, adding phrases like "prompt attention is appreciated" or "time-sensitive" can increase the priority of your request.

Monitoring response timelines also allows you to adjust follow-up communications effectively. If a creditor promised a response within a certain timeframe and failed to deliver, mention the missed deadline in your follow-up message. Phrasing like, "I am following up on my previous request, which I expected by [date]," reinforces accountability and sets an expectation for timely action.

7. Use Data from Previous Interactions to Fine-Tune Requests

The effectiveness of the 11 Magic Words improves with each interaction as you gather data on what works best with specific creditors or agencies. Over time, you'll begin to see patterns in which words or combinations elicit the most positive responses. Use this information to tailor future communications, incorporating the language that has proven successful in similar contexts.

For instance, if previous requests for "verification" resulted in prompt and accurate responses, continue using this word when addressing similar issues. However, if terms like "confirm" yielded vague or insufficient replies, consider replacing them with stronger alternatives. This iterative approach allows you to continually refine your strategy, maximizing the impact of the 11 Magic Words based on real-world feedback.

8. Periodically Review and Refine Your Approach

Language strategies that are effective initially may need periodic adjustments to remain impactful. Set regular intervals—such as quarterly or semi-annually—to review your communications log and evaluate the success of each interaction. Look for areas where responses could have been clearer, faster, or more comprehensive, and identify ways to refine your language to achieve better results.

This ongoing review process allows you to stay adaptable and responsive to changes in how creditors or agencies interact with you. As you gain more experience with the 11 Magic Words, your approach will become increasingly sophisticated, allowing you to maximize their impact across various situations. Over time, this consistent refinement ensures that your language remains sharp, targeted, and highly effective in achieving your credit management goals.

Maximizing Impact Through Informed Strategy Adjustments

The effectiveness of the 11 Magic Words depends on how thoughtfully they are applied and adapted. By setting clear objectives, monitoring response patterns, adjusting tone, escalating language when necessary, and regularly reviewing your approach, you create a dynamic, results-oriented strategy that leverages the full power of these words. Each adjustment you make not only enhances the immediate interaction but builds a foundation of language skills that strengthen your long-term credit management capabilities. With these guidelines, you can ensure that your use of the Magic Words remains precise, powerful, and tailored to deliver maximum impact in every credit-related interaction.

Chapter 5
Conclusion: Language and Credit – A New Tool of Empowerment

5.1 How to continue leveraging language to build a positive credit history.

As you close this chapter on the 11 Magic Words and their potential to reshape your credit interactions, it's essential to view language not just as a tool but as an ongoing strategy for maintaining and strengthening your credit profile. Building a positive credit history is a continuous process, and the language you use in communication with creditors and credit agencies remains a powerful lever in that journey. The purpose of these strategies is not only to address immediate credit concerns but also to create a foundation for long-term financial empowerment.

By consistently using precise, respectful, and assertive language, you're taking control of your financial narrative. Each interaction, whether it's a routine inquiry, a clarification, or a negotiation, offers an opportunity to reinforce your standing as a responsible and informed borrower. This section explores how to sustain and expand the impact of strategic language, ensuring that your credit history reflects your commitment to financial responsibility and growth.

Developing a Habit of Proactive Communication

One of the best ways to build a positive credit history is through proactive communication. Rather than waiting for issues to arise, make it a habit to reach out periodically to creditors to confirm account details, review payment schedules, or even discuss potential credit increases. These preemptive steps demonstrate your dedication to managing your credit responsibly, showing creditors that you are engaged and proactive.

When engaging in these proactive conversations, continue to use the language principles discussed throughout this book. For instance, phrasing a check-in as, "I'd like to verify that my account details are up to date" or "Could you confirm my current balance and payment schedule?" reinforces your attentiveness to accuracy and responsibility. This approach signals to creditors that you are serious about maintaining good standing and interested in upholding a relationship of mutual respect and transparency.

Reinforcing Accountability in All Credit Transactions

Accountability is one of the cornerstones of a solid credit history. Consistently using language that emphasizes accountability not only keeps your records accurate but also builds trust with creditors and credit bureaus. As you engage in credit transactions, whether it's applying for new credit, requesting a limit increase, or discussing terms, use words that indicate transparency and responsibility, such as "confirm," "accurate," and "documentation."

For example, when opening a new line of credit, ask the representative to "confirm the terms in writing," and after making significant payments, request a "statement update to ensure accuracy." By fostering accountability on both sides of the transaction, you are more likely to avoid misunderstandings or discrepancies in your credit report. This careful, consistent approach reflects positively in your profile, as credit agencies recognize and reward individuals who actively work to maintain clarity and accountability.

Utilizing Language as a Defense Against Potential Errors

Errors on credit reports are more common than many realize, and they can have lasting negative impacts if left unaddressed. Strategic language serves as an effective defense mechanism, allowing you to address and correct inaccuracies swiftly and efficiently. By maintaining an assertive yet respectful tone, you can navigate the dispute process more effectively, ensuring that any issues are resolved in a way that upholds the integrity of your credit history.

For instance, if you spot an error, phrases like, "I respectfully request immediate verification of this entry" or "Please provide supporting documentation to substantiate this report" convey seriousness and demand action. Should the issue require further escalation, adapting your language to be more assertive, such as "Immediate attention to this matter is required to maintain accuracy," demonstrates your commitment to a clear, accurate credit profile. This proactive stance doesn't just resolve individual issues; it reinforces your vigilance in safeguarding your credit history.

Building a Consistent Record of Professionalism

Each communication with creditors contributes to a growing record of how you manage credit. Maintaining a consistent tone of professionalism and clarity builds a reputation with credit agencies and creditors alike, positioning you as a reliable and responsible borrower. Over time, this record of professionalism can influence how these institutions respond to your requests, leading to faster resolutions and, in some cases, more favorable terms.

As you continue to communicate with creditors, make it a priority to use the 11 Magic Words in ways that reinforce this professionalism. For example, when following up on an agreement or clarification, statements like, "Could you kindly confirm that my account reflects the recent changes?" or "I appreciate your assistance in verifying the details of my agreement" project both respect and diligence. This tone fosters positive relationships, potentially paving the way for benefits like lower interest rates, flexible repayment options, or goodwill adjustments.

Embracing Language as Part of Financial Education

One of the most empowering aspects of using language effectively in credit management is that it's a skill that deepens your financial education. As you continue to apply these principles, you'll become more adept at recognizing patterns in credit interactions and anticipating potential issues. Each experience with creditors adds to your knowledge, reinforcing your confidence and capabilities in managing your credit profile independently.

By viewing language as a component of your financial literacy, you gain a more comprehensive understanding of credit management. Each successful interaction not only enhances your credit profile but also strengthens your grasp of financial terminology and procedures. This knowledge becomes a foundation for making informed decisions in other areas of your finances, as you apply similar language strategies to negotiate terms, clarify agreements, and advocate for your interests in diverse financial contexts.

Celebrating Progress and Remaining Adaptable

Building a positive credit history is a gradual process, and each improvement is worth acknowledging. Celebrating these milestones keeps you motivated and focused, reinforcing the value of your efforts. Over time, as you notice the cumulative effects of consistent, precise language, you'll see how small actions build up to create significant improvements in your credit standing.

However, as with any strategy, flexibility is key. The financial landscape evolves, and creditors may change their policies or responses over time. By remaining adaptable in your approach, continuously evaluating the effectiveness of your language, and adjusting as necessary, you'll ensure that your credit management strategy remains relevant and powerful. Adapting to these changes doesn't mean overhauling your approach; often, it's a matter of fine-tuning your phrasing or approach to maintain alignment with current practices.

Concluding Thought: Language as a Lasting Tool of Empowerment

As you close this book, recognize that the 11 Magic Words are more than just a set of terms—they are tools of empowerment. By learning to harness language effectively, you are equipping yourself with a lifelong skill that transcends credit management and applies to all areas of personal finance. The words you choose, the tone you set, and the precision you bring to each interaction have the power to shape your financial future, building a foundation of credibility, accountability, and confidence.

In the journey to strengthen your credit and financial independence, let language be your ally. Each interaction with creditors, each adjustment to your approach, and each success you achieve are reflections of your dedication to taking control of your credit narrative. With these strategies, you're not only improving your credit score but also cultivating a reputation of integrity, responsibility, and empowerment—qualities that will serve you well throughout your financial life.

Made in United States
Cleveland, OH
16 May 2025